OXFORD WORLD'S CLASSICS

THE HOMERIC HYMNS

MICHAEL CRUDDEN teaches Classics at Alexandra College, Dublin.

OXFORD WORLD'S CLASSICS

*For over 100 years Oxford World's Classics have brought
readers closer to the world's great literature. Now with over 700
titles—from the 4,000-year-old myths of Mesopotamia to the
twentieth century's greatest novels—the series makes available
lesser-known as well as celebrated writing.*

*The pocket-sized hardbacks of the early years contained
introductions by Virginia Woolf, T. S. Eliot, Graham Greene,
and other literary figures which enriched the experience of reading.
Today the series is recognized for its fine scholarship and
reliability in texts that span world literature, drama and poetry,
religion, philosophy and politics. Each edition includes perceptive
commentary and essential background information to meet the
changing needs of readers.*

OXFORD WORLD'S CLASSICS

═══

The Homeric Hymns

═══

Translated with an Introduction and Notes by
MICHAEL CRUDDEN

OXFORD
UNIVERSITY PRESS

OXFORD

UNIVERSITY PRESS

Great Clarendon Street, Oxford OX2 6DP

Oxford University Press is a department of the University of Oxford.
It furthers the University's objective of excellence in research, scholarship,
and education by publishing worldwide in

Oxford New York

Auckland Bangkok Buenos Aires Cape Town Chennai
Dar es Salaam Delhi Hong Kong Istanbul Karachi Kolkata
Kuala Lumpur Madrid Melbourne Mexico City Mumbai Nairobi
São Paulo Shanghai Singapore Taipei Tokyo Toronto

with an associated company in Berlin

Oxford is a registered trade mark of Oxford University Press
in the UK and in certain other countries

Published in the United States
by Oxford University Press Inc., New York

© Michael Crudden 2001

Database right Oxford University Press (maker)

First published 2001
First published as an Oxford World's Classics paperback 2002

British Library Cataloguing in Publication Data

Data available

Library of Congress Cataloging in Publication Data

Homeric hymns. English.
The Homeric hymns/translated with an introduction, notes, and glossary of names by
Michael Crudden.

p. cm.
Includes bibliographical references.
ISBN 0-19-280240-2

1 3 5 7 9 10 8 6 4 2

Printed in Great Britain by
Clays Ltd, St Ives plc

For my parents

PREFACE

THE *Homeric Hymns* have always been overshadowed by the *Iliad* and *Odyssey*. Many people today are familiar, at least by repute, with the two great epics and can associate them with a blind bard called Homer, but few are aware that other poems have survived that were attributed to Homer in ancient times. The *Hymns* deserve an audience, even if the gods whom they honour no longer receive worship; I hope that through this translation they will become more widely known. I have tried to be faithful to the Greek text, to achieve clarity of expression, and to produce metrical verse. If the result is useful to students of the Classics, ancient religion, and mythology, and also attractive to the general reader, I shall be content.

I owe large debts of gratitude to many people: to Professor J. M. Dillon, my supervisor as a graduate student; to Professor G. L. Huxley, who has shown a kind interest in my work and given me the benefit of his wise comments on it; to the anonymous Readers of Oxford University Press, who made shrewd observations on the translation and passed on valuable hints for its improvement; to Ms Hilary O'Shea of Oxford University Press, for her willingness to persist with this project; to Miss Enid Barker of Oxford University Press, for her care in supervising the transition from typescript to published volume; to Dr M. J. Clarke, who generously applied his formidable expertise to the typescript, saving me from much foolishness and error, and making many astute suggestions; to Mr P. Gavin, for judicious and insightful remarks as the work evolved; to colleagues and students in Alexandra College, Dublin; to former colleagues and students in St Patrick's College, Maynooth; and to many others. Despite all the friendly and learned counsel available to me, there doubtless remain mistakes and infelicitous expressions in the pages that follow: for these I alone am responsible.

M.C.

CONTENTS

INTRODUCTION

1. BACKGROUND

The poems in this collection belong to the tradition of Greek poetry linked to the name 'Homer'. Not only do manuscripts preserving the *Hymns* name Homer as their author, but Thucydides, an historian of the fifth century BC, attributes to Homer verses that he quotes from *Hymn 3 (To Apollo)*.[1] Yet even in antiquity there were those who claimed that many 'Homeric' poems were not by Homer, and that the great epics *Iliad* and *Odyssey* had different authors.[2] Today 'the *Hymns* of Homer' are judged to be the work of various poets, most of whom were active within the seventh and sixth centuries BC. These hymnists were familiar with both *Iliad* and *Odyssey*, which are usually dated to the eighth century BC; in addition, some (if not all) were acquainted with the poetry of Hesiod, Homer's main rival as the greatest early Greek poet, who may have lived *c.*700 BC. While the *Hymns* can certainly be enjoyed in isolation, the reader is recommended to study them in conjunction with the *Iliad* and *Odyssey*, and also with Hesiod's *Theogony* and *Works and Days* (all of which are available in translation in the Oxford World's Classics series published by Oxford University Press).

The two great epics are the culmination of a long tradition of oral poetry, in which successive generations of singers created verse without the aid of writing (the latter art being unknown in Greece in the 'Dark Age' between *c.*1150 and 800 BC). While it is

[1] The order of the *Hymns* in the translation is that followed by Allen (1912) and most subsequent editors, and is derived from the usual sequence in the manuscripts. As several gods have more than one hymn in their honour, I refer to the *Hymns* by number throughout; when other writers refer, without adding a number, to Homeric hymns in honour of Demeter, Apollo, Hermes, and Aphrodite, they will normally mean the long hymns to these gods (*Hymns* 2, 3, 4, and 5 respectively).

[2] Apart from the *Iliad* and *Odyssey*, several other early Greek epics were attributed to Homer (e.g. *Thebais, Epigonoi, Kypria*), but only fragments of these now survive. See the entry under *Epic Cycle* in *The Oxford Classical Dictionary* (Hornblower and Spawforth 1996: 531), and Evelyn-White (1914: 480–539).

disputed whether the epics themselves as we have them are entirely products of oral composition, the *Hymns* show certain departures from the norms of the *Iliad* and *Odyssey* that are thought to reflect a shift towards literacy. The hymnists are, however, the direct and immediate inheritors of the tradition that gave birth to the *Iliad* and *Odyssey*, and in most respects follow its usages closely. This is especially evident in the *Hymns'* formulaic nature, whether on the level of the individual phrase or in the structuring of entire scenes: repetition, usually faulted in literary works, is essential to the poetic process in works emerging from an oral tradition. The formulaic character of Homeric verse offers fluency in composition, but without narrowly restricting what a talented poet can achieve. Although not operating on the same vast scale as the poet or poets of the *Iliad* and *Odyssey*, the hymnists are skilful enough to profit from their Homeric inheritance, adapting formulae to their own ends and exploiting traditional patterns instead of being confined by them.

Although it is convenient to use the term 'hymnists' to denote the authors of the *Hymns*, these poets are likely not to have devoted themselves exclusively to hymnic composition, but to have been equally proficient in various other types of poetry—most notably heroic epic, of which the *Iliad* and *Odyssey* are the outstanding examples. They were probably itinerant professionals making their living from their poetic recitations (see *Hy.* 3. 174–6),[3] and may have sung or chanted their verses to the strumming of a lyre. The full range of contexts in which they performed is unknown, but included poetic competitions held at religious festivals (see *Hy.* 3. 140–76, *Hy.* 6. 19–20, *Hy.* 26. 12–13). The word *hymnos* or 'hymn', which came to be reserved for poems in honour of gods, seems to have been originally applicable to a poem of any sort, and may have this general sense even in the *Hymns* themselves. Thucydides (3. 104) describes *Hymn* 3 as a *prooimion*, a 'prelude': the implication, supported by the way in which many of the *Hymns* end, is that they offered a way of piously opening a recitation, and that the singer would move on to a more substantial and unrelated piece, perhaps on a heroic

---

[3] *Hy.* = *Hymn*.

theme (see Explanatory Notes on *Hy*. 2. 495). Appropriately, most of the thirty-three surviving hymns (undoubtedly there were many more that are no longer extant) are short, fifteen containing less than ten verses, while only six exceed twenty-five verses in length; but four of this latter group, *Hymns* 2–5, contain narratives rivalling in length and quality individual episodes of the *Iliad* or *Odyssey*, and the question arises whether they could have served as mere preludes.[4] It might be argued that the more important the circumstances in which the poet was reciting, the more elaborate his hymnic prelude would have to be; however, the hymn itself was sometimes the focus of competition, in which case it may not have functioned as a prelude at all (see Explanatory Notes on *Hy*. 3. 540–3). In a couple of instances long and short versions of the same hymn have been preserved (*Hymns* 2 and 13, 4 and 18), possibly reflecting changes in the context for performance. It is likely that many of the shorter hymns are abridged versions of longer hymns that are now lost to us (Parker 1991: 1, 14).

2. STRUCTURE[5]

The most basic structural elements of the *Hymns* can be seen in the shortest specimen, *Hymn* 13 (*To Demeter*), which consists of merely an introduction and conclusion:

> With fair-tressed Demeter, the sacred goddess, my song begins,
> With herself and also her daughter, Persephoneia most fair.
>> Farewell, goddess! Keep this city safe, and begin the song.

The name of the deity at whom the hymn is aimed is prominent in the opening, very often being the first word in the Greek text (as 'Demeter' is in this example, the word-order having been changed in translation). The name is almost always accompanied by epithets relating to the deity's beauty, power, majesty, or

---

[4] *Hymn* 1 should be considered together with *Hymns* 2–5. Now fragmentary, it was originally much longer than its surviving twenty-one verses, as it undoubtedly contained a myth of Dionysos related at length (what the myth was is uncertain, but see the Explanatory Notes on *Hymn* 1).

[5] See Janko (1981) for a more detailed analysis of the *Hymns*' structure.

other qualities (here Demeter is 'fair-tressed', 'sacred'). To identify and glorify the deity further, familial relationships—to parents, siblings, offspring, or a spouse—may be mentioned (in the above example the deity's child is joined with her mother as the subject of the hymn; more typical would be *Hy.* 12. 1, 'Of Hera . . . *whom Rhea bore*'). At the end comes the parting salutation ('Farewell, goddess!'), often with a prayer or plea for favour ('Keep this city safe') and a transition to the poet's succeeding recitation ('begin the song').

The poet can elaborate the introduction further by invoking the Muse or Muses to sing of the chosen deity (e.g. *Hy.* 31. 1–2, *Hy.* 32. 1–2), and by piling up the deity's epithets (as at *Hy.* 28. 2–4). Greater expansion occurs when the hymn acquires a short middle section, in which the deity's qualities, powers, status, achievements, favourite haunts, or pastimes are described or illustrated in a characteristic scene (e.g. the picture of Pan wandering, hunting, making music, and dancing at *Hy.* 19. 8–26, or that of Artemis hunting and dancing at *Hy.* 27. 4–18). The poet may also introduce a brief story, often relating to the deity's birth (e.g. Pan's at *Hy.* 19. 27–47, or Athena's at *Hy.* 28. 4–16). Maximum expansion occurs when a narrative involving the deity is recounted at length. Compare *Hy.* 13 above with *Hy.* 2. 1–3, where the poet moves directly from the introduction into the complex mythic narrative of Persephone's abduction by Hades via a relative clause:

> With fair-tressed Demeter, the sacred goddess, my song begins,
> With herself and her slim-ankled daughter, *whom Aïdoneus once Abducted* . . .

The transition to the middle section of the hymn is usually marked by a relative clause in this way (Janko 1981: 10–11), though it has not always been possible, or seemed effective in English, to retain the relative pronoun at these points in the translation. At the end of the mythic narrative, but before the hymn's conclusion, there may be a 'prolongation' (Janko 1981: 14–15), in which the poet moves from past actions to the deity's present power and glory (e.g. *Hy.* 2. 485–9; compare also *Hy.* 3. 143–64).

3. THE LONG HYMNS[6]

The same basic pattern can be seen to underlie the narratives of the longer hymns. At the beginning something happens that disrupts the existing order of the universe and poses at least a potential threat to the rule of Zeus; by the end a new order has been established, the rule of Zeus is secure once more, and, quite incidentally, the lowly race of humans is better off. This pattern is most clear in *Hymn* 2 (*To Demeter*), where Hades, king of the dead, abducts as his bride Persephone, daughter of the goddess of agriculture, Demeter. Zeus (who is brother of Hades and Demeter, Persephone's father, and king of the gods) had given his consent, though neither the bride nor her mother were informed in advance. Grieving and angered at the unexpected loss of her daughter to the underworld, Demeter withdraws from the gods. The crops stop growing, famine brings the race of mortals to the brink of extinction, and the gods are about to be 'robbed of their glorious due Of portions of honour and offerings' (311–12). The threat of this loss forces Zeus to arrange Persephone's return to her mother. Having eaten food given to her by Hades, Persephone must spend one-third of each year in the underworld; nevertheless, Demeter is satisfied and ends her wrath.

By the end of the poem the breach caused by Persephone's abduction has been healed, and a new order is established, in which Hades keeps his bride, yet the upper world does not for ever lose Demeter's daughter, whose presence is necessary for life and growth. Demeter and her child return to Olympos, 'having their dwelling there by Zeus whom thunder delights' (485). Humans, once recovered from their famine, can resume making the offerings that the gods crave, but also gain a blessing that they had not previously enjoyed. For after withdrawing from the gods Demeter had not immediately stopped the crops from growing; instead, she had wandered long over the earth, and in disguise had entered the service of Keleos, king of Eleusis, as

[6] On the longer hymns I have found the work of Clay (1989) to be particularly enlightening.

nurse of his infant son. She had tried to make the child immortal, but the mortal stupidity of his mother Metaneira foiled the attempt. All was not lost, however, as Demeter taught the leaders of Eleusis how to perform rites in her honour. Those who worship her duly by participating in them will gain a great boon. Not only will they enjoy increased material prosperity, they will even have a better lot in the afterlife than the uninitiated (480–2):

> Blessed is he who has seen them of humans who walk on the earth;
> But he who has not been enrolled in the rites, who is lacking a share,
> In death has no matching portion down in the mouldy gloom.

This is the origin of the Eleusinian Mysteries, the most famous of the many mystery cults in Ancient Greece that offered to initiates consolation against mortality.

In *Hymn* 3 (*To Apollo*) there is a similar movement from divine conflict to the present position in which the condition of humans is improved. Zeus has committed adultery with Leto, who becomes pregnant; his jealous wife Hera, to prevent Leto from giving birth, detains Eileithyia, the goddess of birth, on Olympos; the other goddesses secretly bribe Eileithyia to come to the island of Delos, where Leto in her prolonged labour waits, and Apollo at last is born.

Leto had found it difficult to discover a place in which to give birth, as a malicious rumour had spread abroad that her son would be reckless and violent, an oppressive tyrant to gods and humans (66–73); but Apollo, far from menacing the established order of the universe with his strength, in his first utterance subordinates himself to Zeus (132), and later kills the huge Snake allied to his father's enemies that lurks in the vicinity of Delphi (302–4):

> a savage monster, who caused
> Much harm to humans on earth—much harm to humans themselves,
> And much to their slender-legged flocks, since she was a blood-
> spattered bane.

But Apollo does not kill the Snake merely out of a sense of duty to his father, nor from philanthropy. Having just laid the foundations near by of his Delphic oracle, he must eliminate this creature that preys both on humans and (more importantly) on the 'slender-legged flocks' that he wants them to sacrifice at Delphi in his honour. Humans do, of course, profit from knowing the will of Zeus as it is mediated to them through Apollo's oracle in return for their offerings; Apollo, however, is a god who punishes wrongdoing, and his human ministers must not forget it (540–3).

In *Hymn* 4 (*To Hermes*) the birth of a son of Zeus again causes a disturbance in the order of the universe. This time Zeus secretly impregnates the mountain nymph Maia with Hermes. Once born, the infant god is not content to remain in obscurity in his mother's cave 'deprived of gifts ' And prayers' (168), but wishes to earn a place amongst the Olympian gods and enjoy the riches that human worship brings. To satisfy this ambition, he steals the cattle of his half-brother Apollo; the latter comes in pursuit of the thief, and hauls the felonious infant before their father Zeus, who, despite ordering Hermes to return the cattle, is delighted by his son's roguish trickery. In the end Apollo and Hermes are reconciled, and Hermes gains all his present powers and privileges together with a place on Olympos.

If Hermes had not been allowed to join the Olympian gods, he would have caused them no end of problems through his skill as a thief—at one point he threatens to break into Apollo's temple at Delphi and rob all the treasures stored up inside (174–81). But even when he is integrated into the divine community, he is not an unmixed blessing as far as humans are concerned. He may grant them knowledge of the future through a form of divination passed on to him by Apollo (552–66); also, in the course of the narrative he creates several inventions—the lyre, sandals, fire-sticks, the syrinx—and devises in addition a procedure for equitably dividing meat, all of which have passed into the human realm, even if Hermes is not said to have transmitted them to us himself. Hermes is exceptional in his ambivalent nature: god of luck, travellers, heralds, merchants, shepherds, and much else, he remains the god of thieves. The poet sums up his activities (576–8):

> With all mortals and immortals both
> He has dealings; seldom though does he help, but unceasingly cheats
> Throughout the gloomy night the tribes of mortal men.

The challenge for humans is to get on the good side of this Trickster god, and to be among the select few of mortals to enjoy his favour. But even those who suffer from his more mischievous activities have to recognize, as Apollo does, how much better life has become through the inventive powers of this quicksilver character.

As the narrative of *Hymn* 5 (*To Aphrodite*) opens, there is a disturbance in the natural order of the universe. Aphrodite, goddess of love, has been flaunting her power for her own amusement by making most of the other gods, including Zeus himself, infatuated with humans: immortals have mated with mortals and produced mortal offspring, and have then been subjected to Aphrodite's mockery at these shameful liaisons (48–52). Zeus stops her scoffing by making her fall in love with a mortal man, the Trojan Ankhises; the result of their union is a mortal son, Aineias. Aphrodite herself now feels the shame of such intimate contact with a lowly human, a shame that she expresses in the very name that she chooses for her son (see Explanatory Notes on *Hy.* 5. 198–9). She will never be able to mock the other gods again as before (247–55), and at the end of the poem she shows her subordination to Zeus by threatening Ankhises with her father's thunderbolt if ever he names her as the mother of their child (288). The hymn ends abruptly with the goddess shooting back up to heaven where she belongs. It is not stated in the poem that the gods will never again mate with humans and produce offspring with them, but the implication at least is that Aphrodite will no longer cause this to happen in the same manner as before, to flaunt her power. If it happens in future, it will be for a different reason, and in accordance with the will of Zeus.

What profit accrues to mortals from the divine conflict in *Hymn* 5? We might say that the human race has been ennobled by an admixture of divine blood, but the benefits of this admixture seem to be confined strictly to Aineias and his descendants (196–7). Despite showing the closest possible contact between mortal and immortal, the poem emphasizes the vast gulf between them. Aphrodite spells out to Ankhises why they can have no long-lasting relationship: old age and death, to which he is subject, will separate them (239–46).

4. THE *HYMNS* AND HUMANS

Although the gods play a major part in the *Iliad* and *Odyssey*, the epics' main focus is on the mortal heroes and their unfolding destinies; in the *Hymns* the human characters are mere bit-players in a drama that redounds to the gods' greater glory. However, when mortals and immortals come into contact in the longer hymns, there is need on both sides: obviously the human need is the more urgent, the human role the humbler, but the gods somehow cannot do without our worship, and will reward us for it. With the gods' favour we may even for a time possess the godlike beauty, strength, grace, and wealth of the Ionians in their Delian festival (*Hy.* 3. 146–64). But despite the benefits that come to us from the gods, it is not forgotten that they give ill as well as good, and we must accept whatever they choose to bestow upon us. As Keleos' daughter Kallidike reminds the disguised Demeter at *Hy.* 2. 147–8,

Mother, the gifts that the gods bestow we humans endure
Perforce, though filled with grief: for they are more mighty by far.

In these words there is no complaint, simply resignation and recognition of facts. The human position in relation to the gods is wretched and lowly: they have eternal youth, everlasting life, and great power, whereas we are weak, short-lived, and subject to old age. This harsh reality is perhaps most manifest in *Hymn* 3, where the poet with perfect detachment summarizes the song that the Muses sing in an Olympian celebration (189–93):

All the Muses with beautiful voices together responsively hymn
The gods' undying gifts and those pains that humans endure
At the hands of immortal gods as they live without wits or resource,
And can find no cure for death or defence against old age.

In the midst of a divine festivity the Muses contrast the immortals' happy lot with the unfortunate plight of humans. The gods seem better able to savour the gifts that they enjoy by contemplating the sort of existence that those who do not possess them must endure. Neither the effect nor the intention of this song is to evoke sympathy amongst them for humans: they delight in their dancing, despite the fact that the theme of their music is the mortal suffering that they themselves have caused. The tone of the verses is not even neutral, but actually scornful of humans, as if they are to blame for being stricken with age and death—the weak deserving the contempt of the strong. In the two Homeric epics the gods are also responsible for human sufferings, but a motive is assigned to them: these sufferings will give future generations of humans themes for song, and on entering the fray the hero can console himself with the thought that his glorious death will be celebrated and his memory preserved for ever (*Iliad* 6. 357–8; *Odyssey* 8. 579–80). Yet in the Muses' song, the apogee of poetry, our failure is contemptible, not glorious.

Inscribed on Apollo's temple at Delphi were two admonitions: 'Know Yourself' and 'Nothing to Excess'. Those approaching the god are forced to remember that they are only human, and must not exceed due measure lest they incur divine wrath. The *Hymns* offer a similar warning, and one that may have been more timely, if indeed they were preludes to epic recitations on the splendid deeds of mortal heroes. They remind the audience at the outset of song of the true nature of things, in which we are, from the lofty perspective of Olympos, so insignificant.

NOTE ON THE TRANSLATION

THE ideal translation expresses the meaning and nuances of the original text using the same number of words in the same order and grammatical sequence and with the same effects of sound and rhythm—in other words, the ideal translation is unattainable. Even a prose translation into English of a Greek prose original cannot follow at all points both the word-order and grammatical structure of the Greek, for Greek (like Latin) is an inflected language in which word-order is much less restricted than in English. Additional complications arise when Greek poetry is being translated into English verse. A phrasing in English that suitably conveys the sense will not necessarily be metrical. 'Free verse' allows a way of escape, but certain words and expressions were not available to the Greek poets due to the unyielding demands of their metres, and verse translators should operate under similar constraints.

Homeric poetry is composed in a fixed metre, called the dactylic hexameter catalectic. This, like most Classical metres, is quantitative, which means that it is based on patterns of long (–) and short (∪) syllables. The verse in this metre is divided into six 'feet', the first four of which may be either dactyls (a dactyl = – ∪ ∪) or spondees (a spondee = – –); the fifth foot is normally a dactyl; the sixth and final foot is 'catalectic', i.e. stopping short, being either a trochee (– ∪) or a spondee, but never a dactyl. The other main feature of the verse is the caesura, an emphatic pause between words within a foot, most often the third.

If possible, a poetic translation ought to use the same metre as the original text. However, since poetry in English is not quantitative, but instead uses patterns of stressed (ˈ) and unstressed (∪) syllables, an English translation cannot reproduce the metrical effects of the Greek. Even if we regard a stressed syllable as the equivalent in English of a long Greek syllable, and an unstressed syllable as the equivalent of a short Greek one, we cannot mimic the Greek verse successfully, because the spondee in English is two consecutive stressed syllables, and the foot following a spondee would itself have to begin with yet another stressed syllable, so that the use of a single spondee in a verse would entail three successive stressed syllables. This would be difficult to achieve in a pleasing way.

The metre of this translation has six beats or stressed syllables in each verse, corresponding to the six feet of the Greek verse. One stressed syllable is separated from the next by either one or two unstressed syllables. The verse usually begins with an unstressed syllable, though sometimes for variety the first syllable is stressed; consequently, the normal rhythm is iambo-anapaestic, but may become trochaeo-dactylic. The reason why a mostly iambo-anapaestic rhythm was chosen is that the iamb (˘ˈ) is the standard metrical unit in English, and its natural expansion is the anapaest (˘˘ˈ). There is often an emphatic pause between the third and fourth stressed syllables, representing the Greek caesura. The verse normally ends on a stressed syllable. *Hy*. 1. 1–3 will serve to illustrate:

> ˘   ˈ   ˘ ˘   ˈ   ˘   ˈ ˘ ˘   ˈ ˘ ˘   ˈ   ˘ ˘   ˈ
> For some say it was on Drakanon; Ikaros swept by the wind,
>
> ˘   ˈ   ˘   ˈ   ˘   ˈ   ˘   ˈ   ˘   ˈ   ˘   ˈ
> Say others; others, Naxos, brilliant, insewn child;
>
> ˈ   ˘ ˘   ˈ   ˘ ˘   ˈ ˘   ˘ ˘ ˈ ˘   ˘   ˈ   ˘   ˘   ˈ
> Some, that it was by Alpheios, the river whose eddies swirl deep . . .

Translators into a fixed metre inevitably face certain temptations, one of which is to pad. Although sometimes succumbing (mainly to avoid inappropriate beginnings and endings in mid-verse, and to accommodate awkward proper names to my metre), I have tried to resist. The result is that the sense is usually expressed in fewer verses than in the original: in total, 2,332 Greek verses have yielded 2,168 English. To facilitate reference to the Greek text, its line-numbers are given in the margin of the translation (the number given is that of the Greek verse containing the word to which the *last* word of the verse in the translation corresponds).

In the spelling of proper names I have usually transliterated directly from the Greek, eschewing 'c', '-us', and other features of Latinization except for the use of 'y' (e.g. 'Khimaira' is written instead of 'Chimaera', 'Kronos' instead of 'Cronus', 'Polyxeinos' instead of 'Polyxenus'), though in some cases I have preferred a more familiar Greek but non-Homeric form (e.g. 'Hera' instead of 'Here'). Occasionally, however, Latinized or Anglicized forms (e.g. 'Cyprus', 'Egypt') proved too familiar, metrically useful, or aurally pleasing to abandon. If the spelling of a name in the translation differs significantly from that in the Greek text, this will be explained in the Glossary of Names.

The *Hymns*, like most of Classical literature, survived to modern times by being copied out manually again and again over the centuries. This process, while it ensured their survival, introduced errors and blemishes. In the translation a line of spaced full points denotes a lacuna, where one or more verses are thought to have been lost in the course of the text's transmission. At *Hy*. 2. 387–404 and 462–79, where the manuscript that preserves the Greek text is torn, I use square brackets to give a rough indication of the damage, and enclose within square brackets any conjectural supplements that seem likely to be correct. As this volume is not intended to serve as a critical edition, the discussion of textual problems in the Explanatory Notes has been kept to a minimum.

The translation does not adhere in every particular to any one edition of the Greek text. Allen's (1912) has been taken as basic, except for *Hymn* 2, where it yields place to Richardson's (1974), but preference has sometimes been given to readings and conjectures that were adopted by Càssola (1975) or appear in his apparatus criticus. In the task of interpretation the commentaries of Allen, Halliday, and Sikes (1936), Richardson (1974), and Càssola (1975) offered invaluable assistance, as did the study of the *Hymns* by Clay (1989); also indispensable were the various works of M. L. West and R. Janko that are listed in the Bibliography. The translations of the *Hymns* into French, German, and Italian by Humbert (1936), Weiher (1989), and Càssola (1975) respectively were another reliable and welcome source of help in moments of perplexity. To avoid undue influence on my choice of vocabulary and phrasing, I decided

at the outset not to consult English-language translations of the
Hymns, though Evelyn-White's work (1914) was already familiar
to me from previous study;[1] at relevant points, however, I did
consult translations into English of other works, and found
particularly instructive W. Shewring's translation of the *Odyssey*
and M. L. West's of Hesiod's *Theogony* and *Works and Days* (both
published by Oxford University Press in the Oxford World's
Classics series). In preparing this book I have incurred an
incalculable debt to the work of numerous scholars, past and
present, that the Bibliography and Explanatory Notes cannot
begin to acknowledge.[2]

[1] English-language translations of the *Hymns* published in recent decades include
those of A. N. Athanassakis (Baltimore: The Johns Hopkins Univ. Press, 1976), C. Boer
(Chicago: The Swallow Press, 1970), T. Sargent (New York: Norton, 1973), and S. C.
Shelmerdine (Newburyport, Mass.: Focus Information Group, 1995); in addition, *Hymn*
2 has been translated by H. P. Foley (*The Homeric Hymn to Demeter: translation, commentary
and interpretative essays*, Princeton: Princeton Univ. Press, 1994).

[2] My work was largely completed before the edition by Giuseppe Zanetto (*Inni Omerici*,
Milan: Biblioteca Universale Rizzoli, 1996) came to my attention.

SELECT BIBLIOGRAPHY

ALLEN, T. W. (1912), *Homeri Opera, Tomus V* (Oxford: Clarendon Press).

—— HALLIDAY, W. R., and SIKES, E. E. (1936), *The Homeric Hymns* (Oxford: Clarendon Press).

BURKERT, W. (1984), 'Sacrificio-sacrilegio: il "trickster" fondatore', *Studi Storici*, 4: 835–45.

—— (1985), *Greek Religion, Archaic and Classical*, trans. by J. Raffan (Oxford: Basil Blackwell Ltd.).

CÀSSOLA, F. (1975), *Inni Omerici* (Milan: Fondazione Lorenzo Valla, Arnoldo Mondadori Editore).

CLAY, J. STRAUSS (1989), *The Politics of Olympus: Form and Meaning in the Major Homeric Hymns* (Princeton: Princeton University Press).

CLINTON, K. (1993), 'The Sanctuary of Demeter and Kore at Eleusis', in N. Marinatos and R. Hägg (eds.), *Greek Sanctuaries: New Approaches* (London and New York: Routledge), 110–24.

DEUBNER, L. (1938), 'Der homerische Apollonhymnus', *Sitzungsberichte der preußischen Akademie der Wissenschaften*, 24: 248–77.

EDWARDS, M. W. (1991), *The Iliad: A Commentary, Volume V: books 17–20* (Cambridge: Cambridge University Press).

EVELYN-WHITE, H. G. (1914), *Hesiod, the Homeric Hymns and Homerica* (Cambridge, Mass., and London: Harvard University Press and William Heinemann Ltd.).

FARNELL, L. R. (1896–1909), *The Cults of the Greek States*, 5 vols. (Oxford: Clarendon Press).

FERNÁNDEZ DELGADO, J. A. (1990), 'Orakel-Parodie, Mündliche Dichtung und Literatur im homerischen Hermes-Hymnus', in W. Kullmann and R. Reichel (eds.), *Der Übergang von der Mündlichkeit zur Literatur bei den Griechen* (Tübingen: Gunter Narr Verlag), 199–225.

FONTENROSE, J. (1959), *Python: A Study of Delphic Myth and its Origins* (Berkeley: University of California Press).

GÖRGEMANNS, H. (1976), 'Rhetorik und Poetik im homerischen Hermeshymnus', in H. Görgemanns and E. A. Schmidt (eds.), *Studien zum antiken Epos* (Meisenheim am Glan: Verlag Anton Hain), 113–28.

HAINSWORTH, B. (1993), *The Iliad: A Commentary, Volume III: books 9–12* (Cambridge: Cambridge University Press).

HARRISON, J. E. (1903), 'Mystica vannus Iacchi', *Journal of Hellenic Studies*, 23: 292–324.

HEUBECK, A., WEST, S., and HAINSWORTH, J. B. (1988), *A Commentary on Homer's Odyssey, Volume I: Introduction and Books I–VIII* (Oxford: Clarendon Press).

—— and HOEKSTRA, A. (1989), *A Commentary on Homer's Odyssey, Volume II: Books IX–XVI* (Oxford: Clarendon Press).

HOLLAND, R. (1926), 'Battos', *Rheinisches Museum für Philologie*, 75: 156–83.

HORNBLOWER, S., and SPAWFORTH, A. (1996), *The Oxford Classical Dictionary*, 3rd edn. (Oxford and New York: Oxford University Press).

HUMBERT, J. (1936), *Homère: Hymnes* (Paris: Les Belles Lettres).

JANKO, R. (1981), 'The Structure of the Homeric Hymns: A Study in Genre', *Hermes*, 109: 9–24.

——(1982), *Homer, Hesiod and the Hymns: Diachronic Development in Epic Diction* (Cambridge: Cambridge University Press).

——(1986), 'The *Shield of Heracles* and the Legend of Cyncus', *Classical Quarterly*, 36: 38–59.

——(1991), Review of Clay (1989), *Classical Review*, 41: 12–13.

——(1992), *The Iliad: A Commentary, Volume IV: books 13–16* (Cambridge: Cambridge University Press).

JEANMAIRE, H. (1945), 'Le Substantif *hosia* et sa signification comme terme technique dans le vocabulaire religieux', *Revue des études grecques*, 58: 66–89.

KEANEY, J. (1981), '*Hymn. Ven.* 140 and the Use of "ΑΠΟΙΝΑ'', *American Journal of Philology*, 102: 261–4.

KIRK, G. S. (1985), *The Iliad: A Commentary, Volume I: books 1–4* (Cambridge: Cambridge University Press).

——(1990), *The Iliad: A Commentary, Volume II: books 5–8* (Cambridge: Cambridge University Press).

LARSON, J. (1995), 'The Corycian Nymphs and the Bee Maidens of the Homeric *Hymn to Hermes*', *Greek, Roman, and Byzantine Studies*, 36: 341–57.

LIDDELL, H. G., and SCOTT, R. (1940), *A Greek–English Lexicon*, 9th edn., rev. by H. Stuart Jones with R. McKenzie, *with a Revised Supplement*, ed. by P. G. W. Glare with A. A. Thompson 1996 (Oxford: Clarendon Press).

LLOYD-JONES, H. (1996), *Sophocles: Fragments* (Cambridge, Mass., and London: Harvard University Press).

MERKELBACH, R. (1973), 'Ein Fragment des homerischen Dionysos-Hymnus', *Zeitschrift für Papyrologie und Epigraphik*, 12: 212–15.

MILLER, A. M. (1986), *From Delos to Delphi: A Literary Study of the Homeric Hymn to Apollo* (Leiden: E. J. Brill).

PARKER, R. (1991), 'The *Hymn to Demeter* and the *Homeric Hymns*', *Greece and Rome*, 38: 1–17.

PENGLASE, C. (1994), *Greek Myths and Mesopotamia: Parallels and Influence in the Homeric Hymns and Hesiod* (London and New York: Routledge).

RADERMACHER, L. (1931), *Der homerische Hermeshymnus* (Sitzungsberichte der Akademie der Wissenschaften in Wien 213, no. 1: 1–263).

RADIN, P. (1956), *The Trickster: A Study in American Indian Mythology*, with commentaries by K. Kerényi and C. G. Jung (London: Routledge and Kegan Paul).

RICHARDSON, N. J. (1974), *The Homeric Hymn to Demeter* (Oxford: Clarendon Press).

—— (1993), *The Iliad: A Commentary, Volume VI: books 21–24* (Cambridge: Cambridge University Press).

RUSSO, J., FERNÁNDEZ-GALIANO, M., and HEUBECK, A. (1992), *A Commentary on Homer's Odyssey, Volume III: Books XVII–XXIV* (Oxford: Clarendon Press).

SCHACHTER, A. (1976), '*Homeric Hymn to Apollo*, lines 231–238 (The Onchestus Episode): Another Interpretation', *Bulletin of the Institute of Classical Studies of London University*, 23: 102–14.

—— (1994), *Cults of Boiotia, 3: Potnia to Zeus* (London: Institute of Classical Studies, University of London).

SCHEINBERG, S. (1979), 'The Bee Maidens of the Homeric *Hymn to Hermes*', *Harvard Studies in Classical Philology*, 83: 1–28.

SOWA, C. ANGIER (1984), *Traditional Themes and the Homeric Hymns* (Chicago: Bolchazy-Carducci Publishers).

VERMEULE, E. (1979), *Aspects of Death in Early Greek Art and Poetry* (Berkeley: University of California Press).

WALCOT, P. (1991), 'The Homeric *Hymn to Aphrodite*: A Literary Appraisal', *Greece and Rome*, 38: 137–55.

WEIHER, A. (1989), *Homerische Hymnen*, 6th edn. (Munich and Zurich: Artemis Verlag).

WEST, M. L. (1966), *Hesiod: Theogony* (Oxford: Clarendon Press).

—— (1970), 'The Eighth Homeric Hymn and Proclus', *Classical Quarterly*, 20: 300–4.

WEST, M. L. (1975), 'Cynaethus' Hymn to Apollo', *Classical Quarterly*, 25: 161–70.

——(1978), *Hesiod: Works and Days* (Oxford: Clarendon Press).

THE HOMERIC HYMNS

.   .   .   .

For some say it was on Drakanon; Ikaros swept by the wind,
Say others; others, Naxos, brilliant, insewn child;
Some, that it was by Alpheios, the river whose eddies swirl
     deep,
That pregnant Semele bore you to Zeus whom thunder
     delights;
Yet others, lord, state that your birth was at Thebes—but all
     that they say
Is false. You were borne by the Father of men and gods
     himself,
Remote from humans, in secret from Hera whose arms are
     pale.
A towering mountain called Nysa, blooming with forest, stands
Far away from the land of Phoinike, near to Egypt's streams

.   .   .   .

'And for her they will dedicate many gifts within their
     shrines.   10
But as he cut you in three, so humans will always perform
Without fail their perfect hecatombs every third year for you.'
     The son of Kronos spoke, and with dark brows nodded
     assent;
The heavenly locks of the lord in waves then rippled down
From his head untouched by death, and he made great
     Olympos shake.
So said sagacious Zeus, and gave the command with his head.
     Be gracious, insewn god who drive women to madness.
     We bards
Sing of you both when we begin and conclude—it cannot be
That one forgetful of you remembers sacred song.
And so to you farewell, Dionysos the insewn god,   20
And to her whom they call Thyone, your mother Semele, too.   21

Hymn 2: To Demeter

With fair-tressed Demeter, the sacred goddess, my song
    begins,
With herself and her slim-ankled daughter, whom Aïdoneus
    once
Abducted—given to him by deep-crashing, far-seeing Zeus—
While remote from Demeter whose sword is golden, of
    sparkling fruits,
She was joining together with Ocean's full-bosomed daughters
    in play,
And amidst a soft meadow-field was plucking flowers: the
    rose,
The crocus and beautiful violet, iris and hyacinth blooms,
And narcissus—grown by Earth through the will of Zeus to
    please
The Receiver of Many, a snare for the maiden with budding
    face—
A wondrous, radiant blossom, awesome for all to view,   10
Both for immortal gods and also for mortal men.
From this plant's root a hundred heads had sprouted up,
And scent most sweetly spread; all Heaven wide above
Beamed, as did all Earth, and the salty swell of the Sea.
And she, being struck with wonder, reached out with both of
    her hands
To grasp this beautiful plaything; but broad-pathed Earth
    gaped wide
On the Nysion plain where the lord, the Receiver of Many,
    rushed forth
With his deathless horses, Kronos' son who has many a name.
He seized her against her will, and aboard his golden car
Carried her off, lamenting; she uttered a piercing scream   20
In appeal to her father, Kronos' son, the highest and best.
But there was not any amongst the immortals or mortal men
Who heard her call, nor did the olives with sparkling fruit;
Only Persaios' daughter whose thoughts are of youthful mirth,
The brightly head-dressed Hekate, heard from within her cave,
As did the lordly Sun, Hyperion's splendid child,

When the maiden shrieked in appeal to her father, Kronos'
     son.
But Zeus sat apart, far away from the gods, in a prayer-filled
     shrine,
And received the beautiful offerings made by mortal men.
And against her will her father's brother carried her off,   30
The Commander of Many, Receiver of Many, by Zeus' advice
With his deathless horses, Kronos' son who has many a name.
    While the goddess viewed earth and starry sky, and the
      strong-flowing sea
Teeming with fish, and the rays of the Sun, she still hoped to
     behold
Her dear mother again, and the tribes of gods eternal in race;
So long did hope soothe her mighty mind despite her grief
  .   .   .   .

The mountains' peaks and the depths of the sea rang out at
     the sound
Of her deathless voice, and her queenly mother caught the
     cry:
A sharp pain took hold of her heart, and about her heavenly
     locks
She rent her head-dress, cast from her shoulders her dark veil
     down,   42
And over both firm and fluid rushed like a bird in her search;
But there was not any amongst the gods or mortal men
Who would tell her the truth, nor from birds did any true
     messenger come.
For nine days then queenly Deo wandered across the earth,
A flaming torch in each hand, and neither ambrosia touched
Nor sweet-tasting nektar in grief, nor with bath-water splashed
     her flesh.
But when for the tenth time upon her the radiant Dawn had
     shone,
Then she was met by Hekate holding a light in her hands,
Who, to report her tidings, addressed her with words and said:
    'Queen Demeter, Bringer of Seasons, Bestower of
      Splendid Gifts,   54
Who amongst the heavenly gods or mortal men

Carried Persephone off and grieved you within your heart?
For I heard the sound of her voice, yet caught no glimpse with
     my eyes
Of the one who carried her off: I tell you at once the whole
     truth.'
    So Hekate spoke; the daughter of Rhea whose tresses are
     fair
Gave her no answer in speech, but together with her in haste
Rushed onward, holding in each hand a flaming torch.
They came to the Sun, the watcher of gods and men, and
     stood
In front of his horses. The bright one of goddesses questioned
     him:
    'Sun, as a god for a goddess show your regard for me,   64
If ever by word or deed your heart and spirit I pleased.
The daughter whom I bore, my sweet offshoot of glorious
     form,
I heard through the murmuring air giving vent to an
     anguished cry
As though overpowered by force, yet caught no glimpse with
     my eyes.
But since from the brilliant sky you look down on all earth
     and sea
With your rays, now tell me the truth: have you anywhere
     seen my child?
Who took her without my consent against her will by force
And vanished—one of the gods, or was he of mortal men?'
    In this way she spoke, and Hyperion's son responded in
     speech:
'Daughter of fair-tressed Rhea, lady Demeter, you'll know.   76
For indeed I have great respect and pity for you in your grief
Concerning your slim-ankled child. No one else of the gods
     was the cause
Save Zeus who gathers the clouds: to be called his flourishing
     spouse
He gave her to Hades his brother, who snatched her and
     carried her off
Down to the murky gloom with his horses, shrieking loud.

But, goddess, cease your deep mourning—nor must you at all
　　　in vain
Keep hold of boundless rage. A not unsuitable match
Amongst the immortal gods for your daughter to marry is he,
Aïdoneus, Commander of Many, your very own brother by
　　　birth,
Sown from the selfsame seed. And as regards honour, he
　　　gained　　　　　　　　　　　　　　　　　　　　　86
His share by lot at the first, when the three-way division was
　　　made:
He dwells amongst those whose sovereign it fell to his lot to
　　　be.'
　　With that he called to his horses, and at his behest they
　　　began
Quickly to pull the swift car, like birds with their wings
　　　outstretched;
But into the heart of Demeter came grief more dreadful and
　　　grim.
She then was filled with anger at Kronos' black-clouded son,
And forsaking the gods' assembly and tall Olympos mount,
For a long time through humans' cities and rich tilled fields
　　　she went,
Effacing the signs of her beauty; and no one who saw her of
　　　men
Or deep-girdled women knew her, until she came to the
　　　house　　　　　　　　　　　　　　　　　　　　　96
Of shrewd-minded Keleos, sovereign of fragrant Eleusis then.
She sat near the road, her heart full of woe, by the Maiden's
　　　Well,
Where the townsfolk drew water in shade—above it an olive-
　　　bush grew.
She resembled an aged woman born many years before,
Now deprived of the power of birth and the gifts that the
　　　goddess bestows,
Aphrodite the lover of garlands; one such as those who nurse
The children of doom-dealing kings and serve in their echoing
　　　halls.
　　The daughters of Keleos, son of Eleusinos, saw her there,

As they came for the easy-drawn water, to bring it in pitchers
    of bronze
To their father's beloved halls, like four goddesses, blooming
    with youth: 108
Amongst them Kallidike came, Kleisidike too was there,
And Demo the lovely came, and Kallithoe eldest of all.
They did not know her—but hard are gods for mortals to see.
And standing close near by, they addressed her with winged
    words:
    'Who are you, of all the humans born many years ago,
And from where do you come, old woman? And why have
    you taken yourself
Outside the city's bounds, and don't draw near the homes
Where women of your age and younger dwell in the shadowy
    halls
Who would receive you kindly in word and also in deed?'
    So they spoke; and she, a queen amongst goddesses,
    answered with words: 118
'Dear children, whoever you are of female womanhood, hail!
I'll tell you; it's only good manners to answer your questions
    with truth.
My name is *Doso*—my queenly mother called me that.
Yet now from Crete I've come upon the broad back of the sea,
Not willing; with violence, rather, against my will by force
Pirate men carried me off. They beached their swift ship next
At Thorikos; there the women stepped on shore in a throng,
As did the men also themselves. They began to prepare a meal
By the ship's stern-cables; within me, however, I felt no desire
For the honey-sweet savour of supper, but rushing unseen I
    passed   131
In flight from my arrogant masters over the land's black soil,
Lest they sell me—picked up for free—and enjoy the price that
    I'd fetch.
So here I've arrived in my wanderings, having no notion at all
What country this is that I've come to and who its natives are.
But may all who have homes on Olympos grant husbands to
    you and the birth
Of children, as parents wish—but, maidens, take pity on me

.   .   .   .

With a ready mind, dear children: whose house may I
    approach,
The home of what husband and wife, to perform with a ready
    mind
Such tasks for them as belong to a woman past her prime?
I could hold and finely suckle a new-born babe in my
    arms,   141
And could keep an eye on the house; I could strew the
    master's bed
In a nook of the well-built rooms, and could teach the women
    their tasks.'
    The goddess spoke; to her the maiden as yet untamed,
Kallidike, fairest of Keleos' daughters, at once replied:
    'Mother, the gifts that the gods bestow we humans
        endure
Perforce, though filled with grief: for they are more mighty by
    far.
But what you seek to know I'll pass on exactly and name
The men who here possess the great power that honour
    brings,
Who amongst their folk stand first, and guard the town's
    head-dress of walls
By means of their plans and straight judgements: Triptolemos
    shrewd in thought,   153
Dioklos and Polyxeinos, Eumolpos free of fault,
Dolikhos and our brave father—of all these men there are
    wives
Who manage their household affairs, and amongst these wives
    there is none
Who would scorn at first sight your appearance and shut you
    out from her home;
No, they will bid you welcome, for you have the look of a god.
But if you wish, wait here, while we go to our father's halls
And tell Metaneira, our deep-girdled mother, all this right
    through,
In the hope that she asks you to our house, and not to seek
    others' homes.

She has a darling son being reared in the well-built hall,
Whose birth, coming late, answered many a prayer, and was
      greeted with joy.   165
If you were to rear this child, and he reach his measure of
      youth,
It wouldn't be hard for any of female womanhood then
To feel envy on seeing you, such rewards for his rearing she'd
      give.'
     So she spoke; and with her head Demeter nodded assent.
Having filled their bright vessels with water, the maidens bore
      them away,
Exulting. They speedily reached their father's great abode,
And lost no time in telling all they had seen and heard
To their mother; she lost no time in urging them to go
And call Demeter to her, pledging a boundless wage.
And as hinds or heifers in springtime over the meadow
      leap   175
When their hearts are sated with forage, so did the maidens
      sweep
Along the hollowed cart-track, restraining their billowing garb,
And about their shoulders went streaming locks like the
      crocus' bloom.
    They found her, the glorious goddess, beside the road,
      where before
They had left her; without delay to their father's beloved halls
They led her; behind, her heart full of woe, completely veiled,
She followed them; round the goddess' slim feet her dark robe
      swirled.
And soon they reached the halls of Keleos cherished by Zeus,
And crossing the portico found their queenly mother there,
Where she sat alongside a pillar that propped the solid-made
      roof,   186
With her child on her lap, her young offshoot. The maidens
      ran over to her,
But onto the threshold stepped the goddess: the beam of the
      roof
She touched with her head, and filled the doorway with
      heavenly light.

Metaneira was seized with reverence, awe, and pallid fear;
She surrendered her chair to the goddess, and on it she urged
     her to sit.
But Demeter, Bringer of Seasons, Bestower of Splendid Gifts,
Had no desire to sit upon the gleaming chair,
But continued to wait in silence, her beautiful eyes cast down,
Till Iambe who knew her duties set a compact stool
Beside her, and over it threw a fleece of dazzling white.   196
Then, sitting down, the goddess hid herself under her veil;
For a long time bereft of speech she sat full of woe on the stool.
To no one did she give greeting with either a word or sign;
She had no laughter within her, no hunger for food and drink;
But, with longing pining away for her deep-girdled daughter,
     she sat,
Till Iambe who knew her duties with jokes and by mocking
     induced
Queenly and holy Demeter to smile and laugh and be kind;
And Iambe has pleased her temper then too in later times.
Metaneira proffered a goblet that brimmed with honey-sweet
     wine;
With an upward nod she refused it—it was not permitted, she
     said,   207
For her to drink red wine—but bade her to give her instead
A draught of barley and water mixed with tender mint.
She prepared and handed the goddess the potion as she
     required;
And when for the sake of the rite most queenly Deo received

.   .   .   .

Metaneira whose girdle was fair amongst them was first to
     speak:
   'Hail to you, lady, since you, I believe, were not given
     birth
By parents of low estate, but by parents of noble blood:
You've the grandeur and grace in your gaze that doom-dealing
     kings display.
But come, the gifts that the gods bestow we humans endure
Perforce, though filled with grief: for upon our neck lies the
     yoke.   217

But now, since you've made your way here, all I have will be
    yours to command.
Rear me this boy that I'm holding, whose birth, coming late,
    beyond hope,
The immortals conferred upon me in answer to my many
    prayers.
If you were to rear this child, and he reach his measure of
    youth,
It wouldn't be hard for any of female womanhood then
To feel envy on seeing you, such rewards for his rearing I'd
    give.'
    Demeter whose crown is fair then spoke to her in turn:
'And hail to you also, lady; may heaven grant you what is
    good!
With a ready mind I'll take this boy in my care as you bid:
Rear him I shall, and it's not my belief that he'll suffer
    harm   228
Through the folly of mind of his nurse from a spell or the
    cutter of roots,
For I know a strong counter-cut of more might than the cutter
    of wood,
And I know a safeguard that's good to ward off a baneful spell.'
    When so she had spoken, the goddess took to her fragrant
    breast
The boy in her deathless hands, and his mother felt gladness
    at heart.
So in the halls she reared Demophoon, splendid son
Of shrewd-minded Keleos, whom Metaneira whose girdle was
    fair
Had borne, and he grew like a god. Neither tasting then food
    nor milk

   .   .   .   .

With ambrosia she would anoint him, as if he were sprung
    from a god,
Shedding sweet breath upon him, and clasping him to her
    breast.   238
But by night she would keep him concealed in the mighty fire
    like a log,

In secret from his dear parents—it was a great wonder to
    them,
How he grew in advance of his age, and in looks resembled
    the gods.
And then she would have made him free of age and death,
If in her folly of mind Metaneira whose girdle was fair
Had not kept watch in the night and seen from her fragrant
    room.
Shrieking, she beat her breasts in fear about her boy,
Being much misled at heart, and in grief spoke winged words:
    'Demophoon, child that I bore! The stranger keeps you
      concealed
In the blazing fire, and causes me sorrow and wretched
    woe.'   249
    In this way lamenting she spoke, and the bright one of
      goddesses heard.
Demeter whose crown is lovely, filled with anger at her,
Put away from herself on the ground with her deathless hands
    the dear boy—
Whom she, Metaneira, had borne beyond her hope in the
    halls—
Having snatched him up from the fire with dreadful fury at
    heart,
And at the same instant addressed Metaneira whose girdle was
    fair:
    'Ignorant humans, who lack the discernment to know in
      advance
Your portion of good or ill, as one or the other draws near!
Woman, your folly's misled you beyond all chance of a cure.
For let the gods' oath know this, the implacable water of
    Styx,   259
That I would have made your dear boy ever free of death and
    age,
And would have conferred upon him honour that does not
    fade;
But he now has no means of escaping death and the spirits of
    fate.
But an honour that does not fade will always belong to him,

Because he has climbed on my knees and slept in my arms'
        embrace.
And in due season for him, as the years come rolling round,
Together with one another the boys of Eleusis town
Will always wage for ever war and dreadful strife.
I am the goddess Demeter, holder of honour, who is
For immortals and mortals alike the greatest boon and joy. 269
But come now, let the whole people build a great shrine for me,
And an altar to stand beneath it, under the town and sheer
        wall,
Above Kallikhoros spring, upon the projecting hill;
And I myself will lay down for your instruction my rites,
So that then, by performing them piously, you might appease
        my mind.'
    When so she had spoken, the goddess altered her stature
        and form,
Casting old age away, and round about her then
Beauty began to be breathed: a delightful perfume spread
From the fragrant robes that she wore, a radiance shone out
        far
From the goddess' immortal flesh, to her shoulders golden
        hair streamed,   279
And the solid-made house was filled with a light like the
        lightning-flash.
She went from the halls, and at once Metaneira's knees were
        loosed;
For a long time she lay there mute, not even thinking to lift
Her darling boy from the floor. But his sisters caught the
        sound
Of the piteous squall that he raised, and leaped down from
        their well-strewn beds.
Then one, having lifted him up, to her bosom clasped the boy;
Another kindled the fire; and a third on tender feet rushed
To help their mother stand and emerge from her fragrant
        room.
Gathering round, they began to bathe the struggling boy,
Whom they hugged in a loving embrace; but his spirit was not
        soothed,   290

For inferior nurses and nurturers held him now in their grasp.
> Through all the hours of night, though shaking with
> terror, they sought
To appease the glorious goddess; but at the appearance of
> Dawn
They informed wide-ruling Keleos truly of what was
> prescribed
By the fair-crowned goddess Demeter. Calling his numerous
> folk
To the place of assembly, he gave them the order to make a
> rich shrine
And an altar for fair-tressed Demeter upon the projecting hill;
And they at once obeyed him, complied with his word, and
> built
The shrine in the way he prescribed, and it grew by the
> goddess' decree.
> When they finished and ceased from their labour, they
> each set off for home;   302
But gold-haired Demeter sat there, far from all blessed gods,
And, with longing pining away for her deep-girdled daughter,
> she stayed.
On the earth that nurtures many she brought to pass a year
Most dreadful for humans and grim, when the soil made
> sprout no seed,
For Demeter whose crown is lovely was keeping it then
> concealed.
In the fields the oxen were dragging many curved ploughs in
> vain,
And upon the soil to no purpose fell much white barley grain.
And now she would have destroyed the whole of the human
> race
By means of grievous famine, and robbed of their glorious due
Of portions of honour and offerings those with Olympian
> homes,   312
If Zeus had not perceived and taken note in his mind;
And first he stirred into motion Iris whose wings are of gold
To summon fair-tressed Demeter who has a delightful form.
So to Iris he spoke; and she obeyed Zeus, the black-clouded son

Of Kronos, and ran with her feet at speed through the space
　　　between.
Reaching her journey's end at fragrant Eleusis town,
She found within the shrine Demeter the darkly robed;
And Iris, speaking aloud, addressed her with winged words:
　　'Demeter, you're summoned by Father Zeus who knows
　　　deathless schemes
To come amongst the tribes of gods eternal in race.　　　　322
Now don't leave lacking fulfilment the word that I bring from
　　　Zeus.'
　　In this way entreating she spoke, but Demeter paid no
　　　heed.
Then every one of the blessed gods who always exist
The Father dispatched to her, and drawing near in turn
They invited her and offered many most beautiful gifts
And such honours as she might choose amongst the immortal
　　　gods.
But there was not one who was able to change her mind or
　　　intent
As she seethed with anger in spirit: sternly she spurned their
　　　pleas,
For never on fragrant Olympos would she, she told them, set
　　　foot,
Nor make the crop sprout from the earth, till she saw her fair-
　　　faced child.　　　　333
　　When deep-crashing, far-seeing Zeus heard this, to
　　　Erebos then
He sent the Slayer of Argos who bears the rod of gold
To bring Hades round with soft words and holy Persephone
　　　lead
From the murky gloom to the light amongst the other gods,
So that her mother, on seeing her, might desist from her
　　　wrath.
Hermes did not disobey, but speedily hurtled down
At once from Olympos' seat to the hidden places of earth;
And the lord in his halls he discovered seated upon a couch,
And he had his revered spouse by him, though much against
　　　her will,

Since she longed for Demeter, her mother—who had to the
     blessed gods'   345
Unbearable deeds replied by devising her deadly scheme.
The mighty Slayer of Argos stood close near by and said:
    'Hades whose hair is dark, who rule over those who have
      died,
Zeus the Father has ordered that I from Erebos lead
Splendid Persephone out amongst the other gods,
So that her mother, on seeing her, might pull back from the
     wrath
And the dreadful rage that she nurtures against the immortal
     gods.
For she's thought of a monstrous deed, to wear down the
     feeble tribes
Of humans born on earth, concealing the seed in the soil,
And destroying immortals' honours. She nurtures her dreadful
     wrath   354
And does not mix with the gods, but far away she sits
In her fragrant shrine and presides over rocky Eleusis town.'
    In this way he spoke; Aïdoneus, Lord of Those Below,
With his eyebrows signalling pleasure, did not disobey King
     Zeus'
Commands, but speedily urged Persephone shrewd in
     thought:
    'Go, Persephone, now to your dark-robed mother's side,
Keeping within your breast your temper and spirit mild,
And be in no way despondent too much in excess of the rest.
For amongst the immortals you'll find that I'm no unsuitable
     spouse,
Being Father Zeus' own brother. Going there, you'll rule   365
Over all that lives and moves; amidst the immortals you'll
     have
Honours of greatest worth; and vengeance for ever will come
Upon those who act unjustly and fail to appease your heart
By performing your offerings piously, paying you fitting gifts.'
    In this way he spoke, to the joy of Persephone shrewd in
     thought.
She quickly leaped up in delight, but secretly, glancing round,

He gave her to eat a pomegranate's honey-sweet seed, so that
there
By revered Demeter the dark-robed she would not for ever
stay.
Aïdoneus, Commander of Many, in front of a golden car
Then harnessed two deathless horses, and she got on board;
alongside,   377
The mighty Slayer of Argos with reins and whip in his hands
Made the pair race from the halls, and they not unwillingly
flew.
They completed with speed their long journey; the deathless
horses' career
By sea or the water of rivers, by grassy glens or peaks
Was not delayed, but above these they clove the thick mist as
they went.
He brought to a halt the horses where fair-crowned Demeter
remained,
In front of her fragrant shrine; and she, when she saw them,
rushed
As a raving Maenad might down a mountain shaded with
wood.
[From the] other [side] Persephone [   ]
Of her mother down [   ] 388
She bounded [to] run [   ]
And to her [   ]
[   ]
Ceasing [   ]:
    'Child, now tell me, you surely didn't anything [   ]
Of food? Speak out [   ]
For so, ascending [   ]
Beside myself and the Father, [Kronos' black-clouded son,]
You then could have your home, by all [the immortals
esteemed];
But if you partook, you'll return [to the hidden places of
earth]   398
And dwell for one-third of the seasons [   ]
But the other two-thirds by me and [the rest of the deathless
gods.]

When the earth is blooming with every sweet-scented flower of
    spring,
Then from the murky gloom you will once more ascend,
And will be a mighty wonder for gods and mortal men.

.   .   .   .

And the mighty [Receiver of Many] duped you by means of
    what trick?'
    In answer most lovely Persephone spoke to her in turn:
'Mother, for you I shall indeed recount the whole truth.
When the speedy Slayer of Argos as messenger came to me
From the Father, Kronos' son, and the rest of the heavenly
    gods,   408
And passed on the news that he bore—that from Erebos I was
    to go,
In order that you, on seeing me, might desist from the wrath
And the dreadful rage that you nurture against the immortal
    gods—
I at once leaped up in delight, but Hades secretly put
A food as sweet as honey, a pomegranate's seed, in my hand,
And using violence forced me to taste it against my will.
And how he snatched me up and departed, bearing me off
To the hidden places of earth through the cunning plan
    devised
By my father, Kronos' son, I'll recount and tell all as you
    ask.
We were all in the lovely meadow—Leukippe and Phaino were
    there,   418
Elektra, and also Ianthe; Melite, Iakhe too,
Rhodeia, and also Kallirhoe; there was Melobosis too,
With Tykhe, and also Okyrhoe, nymph with budding face;
Khryseïs too, Ianeira, Akaste, Admete too,
Rhodope also, with Plouto; delightful Kalypso was there,
With Styx, and also Ourania; fair Galaxaure was there,
With Pallas the waker of battle, and archeress Artemis too.
We played and plucked fair blossoms, tender crocus mixed
With iris, hyacinth, rose-buds and lilies, a wonder to view,
And narcissus—grown by broad Earth, and resembling the
    crocus' bloom.   428

But as in delight I plucked it, the ground gave way from
    below,
And there the lord, the mighty Receiver of Many, leaped out.
He bore me away in his golden chariot under the ground,
Though much against my will, and I uttered a piercing cry.
In these words for you I've spoken, despite my grief, the whole
    truth.'
    So then, throughout the whole day, at one with each
        other in mind,
They cheered their hearts and spirits much, embracing with
    love,
And their thoughts were turned from sorrow, each taking and
    giving joy.
The brightly head-dressed Hekate came from near at hand,
And lavished fond embraces on holy Demeter's child: 439
Her usher and helper the Lady from this time forward has
    been.
And deep-crashing, far-seeing Zeus as messenger sent to them
The fair-tressed Rhea to lead amongst the tribes of the gods
Demeter the darkly robed, and promised that he would give
Such honours as she might choose amongst the immortal
    gods;
And he signalled assent with a nod, that her daughter would
    make her home
For one-third of the circling year down in the murky gloom,
By her mother passing two-thirds with the rest of the deathless
    gods.
So to Rhea he spoke; and the goddess did not refuse to convey
The message entrusted by Zeus, but setting off at speed   449
Shot down from Olympos' peaks. She reached the Rarion
    plain,
In times past an udder of ploughland bearing the nurture of
    life,
But it bore no nurture now: it stood idle, devoid of all growth,
And kept the white barley concealed, as Demeter the fair-
    ankled planned.
Yet in future it soon would be sprouting with slender ears of
    corn,

As spring came waxing round; on the earth with ears of corn
Would the fertile furrows be burdened, while others lay bound
    in sheaves.
This was the place where first she arrived from the murmuring
    air;
Seeing each other with joy, they exulted within their hearts,
And the brightly head-dressed Rhea spoke to Demeter these
    words: 459
    'Come now, my child, you are called by deep-crashing,
      far-seeing Zeus
Amongst the tribes of the gods: he promised [that he would give]
[Such] honours [as you might choose] amongst the immortal
    gods;
[And he signalled assent with a nod, that your daughter would
    make her home]
[For one-third of the] circling [year down in the murky gloom,]
[But would pass two-thirds by you and the rest of] the
    deathless gods.
[So did he say it would be,] and nodded his head in assent.
[Come then,] my [daughter,] obey, and don't so [implacably
    rage]
At Kronos' black-clouded son; [instead, without delay,]
Make grow for humans [the harvest] that bears the nurture of
    life.'   469
    [In this way she spoke;] and fair-crowned Demeter did
    [not] disobey,
But sent up from the clod-rich ploughland the harvest without
    delay,
And all broad earth was burdened with leaves and blossoms'
    weight.
The goddess Demeter then went and [showed] to the doom-
    dealing kings—
To Triptolemos, chariot-driving Diokles, Eumolpos the strong,
And Keleos leader of peoples—the way to perform her rites,
And disclosed sacred actions to all that can be in no way
    [transgressed,]
Learnt, or divulged, for the tongue is curbed by the gods'
    great awe.

Blessed is he who has seen them of humans who walk on the
     earth;
But he who has not been enrolled in the rites, who is lacking a
     share,   481
In death has no matching portion down in the mouldy gloom.
     But when by the bright one of goddesses all her rites
     were laid down,
They set off for Olympos and entered the concourse of other
     gods.
Having their dwelling there by Zeus whom thunder delights,
They are sacred and held in reverence. Greatly blessed is he
Of humans who walk on the earth whom they in goodwill
     hold dear:
Without delay they send to the hearth of his great abode
Ploutos, the giver of wealth to humans doomed to death.
     But come now, you who preside over fragrant Eleusis'
     land,
Over Paros that waters flow round, and Antron where rocks
     abound,   491
You queenly Bringer of Seasons, Bestower of Splendid Gifts,
Lady Deo, yourself and your daughter, Persephoneia most fair:
In goodwill return for my song life's nurture that pleases the
     heart.
But I will call to my mind both you and another song.   495

HYMN 3: TO APOLLO

I'll remember and not forget Apollo who shoots from afar.
When he comes, a trembling seizes the gods in Zeus' abode;
And, as he approaches near, they all leap up from their seats,
When he stretches his brilliant bow. The only one to remain
By Zeus whom thunder delights is Leto: she loosens the
      string,
The quiver she shuts, and the bow with her hands from his
      strong shoulders takes,
Against his father's pillar to hang from a peg of gold;
Him she escorts to a throne. His father to him gives
A golden goblet of nektar, saluting his own dear son;
Then the other deities sit, and queenly Leto exults   12
At the fact that she gave birth to a bow-bearing, mighty son.
Hail to you, blessed Leto, since splendid children you bore,
Lord Apollo and archeress Artemis—her at Ortygia, him
On Delos' rocky isle, where against a tall mountain you
      leaned,
The mound of Kynthos, hard by the palm at Inopos' streams.
    How shall I sing a hymn of you, whom hymns have in
      every way praised?
For in your honour, Phoibos, on every side the range of song
Is established, upon both the mainland where calves are
      reared and the isles.
But the peaks and topmost ridges of mountains that rear up
      high,
The rivers that on to the sea are flowing, the headlands that
      slope   24
To the sea, and the harbours of ocean, all these are pleasing to
      you.
Or shall I sing in a hymn how you at the first were borne,
A joy for mortals, by Leto, when she had leaned herself
Against the mountain of Kynthos upon the rocky isle,
Upon Delos that waters flow round, and a dark wave on each
      side rose up,
Driven landward by shrill-blowing gales? From there you
      started out,

And over all mortals hold sway. As many folk as Crete
Contains within her, and Athens' country; Aigina isle,
And, famed for its ships, Euboia; Aigai, Eiresiai too,
And, near to the sea, Peparethos; Athos the Thracian
      height,   33
And the topmost peaks of Pelion; Samos the Thracian isle,
And the shadowy mountains of Ida; Skyros, Phokaia too,
The precipitous mount of Autokane; Imbros the firm-founded
      isle,
And mist-enshrouded Lemnos; holy Lesbos—the seat
Of Makar, Aiolos' son—and Khios that lies in the sea,
Sleekest of isles; rugged Mimas, and Korykos' topmost peaks;
Dazzling Klaros too, and sheer Aisagea mount;
Samos with plentiful waters, precipitous Mykale's peaks;
Miletos, Kos—the city where dwell the Meropes folk—
Precipitous Knidos too, and Karpathos swept by the wind;   43
Naxos, and also Paros, and rocky Rhenaia too—
Over so great a distance in labour with him who shoots
From afar went Leto, seeking whether amongst these lands
There was any that would be willing to furnish her son with a
      home.
But they trembled much in fear, and not one dared, despite
Her rich soil, to welcome Phoibos, until queenly Leto set foot
Upon Delos, and, questioning her, gave voice to winged words:
   'Delos, would you be willing to be the seat of my son,
Of Phoibos Apollo, and furnish him with a rich shrine on your
      ground?
There's no one else who'll touch you or do you honour—
      you'll not,   54
I think, abound in cattle or flocks, nor will you bear corn
Or grow an abundance of trees. But if you possess a shrine
Of Apollo who works from afar, all humans, assembling here,
Will bring you their hecatombs: vast beyond telling the steam
      of fat
Will always be shooting upward, and those who possess you
      you'll feed
From a foreigner's hand, since there is no richness beneath
      your soil.'

In this way she spoke; rejoicing, Delos in answer said:
'Most glorious Leto, daughter of mighty Koios, I would
With pleasure welcome the birth of the lord who shoots from
    afar,
For in truth in men's ears I am of dreadfully grim repute,   64
But in this way might gain great honour. But, Leto, this
    rumour that's spread
Abroad is making me tremble; I'll not keep it hidden from
    you.
For someone exceedingly reckless Apollo, they say, will be,
And will mightily govern immortals and mortals doomed to
    die
Throughout the grain-giving earth; and so this dreadful fear
Pervades my mind and heart, that, when he first sees the
    Sun's light,
Holding the isle in dishonour—since stony indeed is my
    ground—
He may with his feet overturn me and thrust me under the
    sea.
There always great waves without ceasing over my head will
    break,
While he will reach some land that is pleasing to him, to set
    up   76
His shrine and wooded groves. But the many-footed beasts
And black seals will make their lairs upon me, homes that will
    be
Secure for lack of people. But if for me you would swear,
Goddess, a mighty oath, that here he will first set up
A most beautiful shrine as an oracle sought by humans, but
    then

.   .   .   .

Over all humans, since he will be known by many a name.'
    In this way she spoke, and Leto swore the gods' great
    oath:
'Now let the Earth know this, and also broad Heaven above,
And the down-dripping water of Styx, which is the blessed gods'
Greatest and most dread oath: here Phoibos will always
    have   87

His fragrant altar and precinct, and will honour you above all.'
   But when she had sworn and taken the oath to its end,
     while the birth
Of the far-shooting lord was bringing to Delos much joy, for
     nine days
And nine nights was Leto pierced by pangs that offered no
     hope.
Every most excellent goddess was present within the isle,
Dione, Rhea, Ikhnaian Themis, with her who groans loud,
Amphitrite, and also the other female immortals—apart
From Hera whose arms are pale, for she sat inside the halls
Of Zeus who gathers the clouds. Eileithyia the bearer of pains
Alone failed to hear, for she sat under gold-coloured clouds   98
Upon Olympos' peak through pale-armed Hera's guile—
She had in envy detained her, since Leto whose tresses are fair
Was then about to give birth to a blameless and mighty son.
But the goddesses sent out Iris from Delos' firm-founded isle
To fetch Eileithyia, to whom they pledged a great necklace,
     strung
With gold threads, nine cubits long; but they told her to call
     her apart
From Hera whose arms are pale, in case she would with her
     words
Turn her aside as she went. But when swift Iris whose feet
Are the winds had heard the instructions they gave, she set off
     at a run,
And quickly traversed the whole intervening space. But
     when   109
She had come to the seat of the gods, sheer Olympos, she
     summoned out
From the hall to the door Eileithyia, and spoke to her winged
     words,
Just as those goddesses ordered who dwell in Olympian
     homes.
She persuaded the heart in her breast, and the two went
     stepping along,
Like timorous doves in their gait. But when upon Delos set
     foot

Eileithyia the bearer of pains, then of Leto labour took hold,
And she felt the wish to give birth. She embraced the palm
    with her arms
And knelt in the soft meadow-field; the Earth beneath her
    smiled;
Her son leaped out in the light, and every goddess exclaimed.
In a holy, pure bath of clear water then you, bright Phoibos,
    they washed;   120
Swaddled you in a white mantle, fine-spun and newly made;
And wound a gold band about you. Apollo whose sword is of
    gold
Was not given suck by his mother, but Themis with deathless
    hands
Served to him nektar and lovely ambrosia. Leto rejoiced
At the fact that she gave birth to a bow-bearing, mighty son.
    But when, Phoibos, you had consumed this food without
        taint of death,
Your struggles then were not confined by bands of gold,
Bindings no longer detained you, but every cord was loosed.
And at once amongst the goddesses Phoibos Apollo said:
    'May the lyre and curving bow be possessions to call my
        own,   131
And for humans let me proclaim the unerring counsel of
    Zeus.'
    With these words he started to stride upon the broad-
        pathed earth,
Phoibos whose hair is unshorn, the god who shoots from afar,
And all the goddesses wondered; all Delos was laden with gold,
As with gladness she watched the child who of Zeus and Leto
    was born,
Because, of the isles and mainland, the god preferred to make
    her
His home, and had greater love for her in his heart. She
    bloomed
As when the mountain's summit with forest flowers blooms.
    But you whose bow is silver, Apollo the far-shooting lord,
Now stepped on rugged Kynthos, now roamed amongst isles
    and men.   142

Many shrines and wooded groves are yours, and yours to hold
     dear
Are all peaks and topmost ridges of mountains that rear up
     high,
And rivers that on to the sea are flowing; but, Phoibos, at
     heart
You delight in Delos the most, where Ionians trailing their
     robes,
With children and wives who are worthy of reverence, gather
     for you.
And they remember and please you with boxing, dancing, and
     song,
Whenever they hold their assembly. Someone then meeting
     them when
The Ionians throng together would say they always exist
Free of death and age; for he would see the grace
That they all possess, and would please his spirit by watching
     the men,   154
Their wives in beautiful girdles, their swift ships and plentiful
     goods.
And there is this great wonder besides, whose fame will never
     die—
The young Delian women, handmaids of him who shoots from
     afar.
When they hymn first Apollo, and Leto with archeress Artemis
     next,
They remember and sing a hymn of the men and women of old,
And charm the tribes of humans. They know how to mimic
     the speech
And the babble that all humans utter—each man would say
     he himself
Was making the sound, their beautiful singing matches so.
     But come now, may Apollo be gracious, and Artemis too!
And hail to all you women! Hereafter remember me,   166
When of earthly humans some stranger suffering trials comes
     here
And inquires: 'Young women, what man do you think is the
     sweetest of bards

That often passes this way, and in whom do you most
    delight?'
Let you all give fine answer of me: 'A blind man he is, and
    dwells
On rugged Khios; all of his songs are hereafter supreme.'
And I shall bring your fame as far as I wander on earth,
To cities of fine habitation where humans have their homes,
And they will believe my report, since it will indeed be the truth.

    But I will not cease to hymn Apollo who shoots from afar,
God of the Silver Bow, whom lovely-haired Leto bore.   178
Lord, you have Lykia, also lovely Meionie's land,
Miletos too, that desirable city beside the sea,
But you reign in might yourself over Delos that waves wash
    round.

    The son of glorious Leto, playing the hollow lyre,
Approaches rocky Pytho in deathless, scented robes;
His lyre delightfully rings beneath the plectrum of gold.
And then he goes to Olympos, speeding like thought from the
    earth,
To the house of Zeus, and enters the concourse of other gods;
At once the minds of immortals turn to the lyre and song.
All the Muses with beautiful voices together responsively
    hymn   190
The gods' undying gifts and those pains that humans endure
At the hands of immortal gods as they live without wits or
    resource,
And can find no cure for death or defence against old age.
But the fair-tressed Graces and cheerful Seasons, with
    Harmony, Youth,
And the daughter of Zeus, Aphrodite, hold hands by the wrist
    and dance.
Along with them is singing one neither ugly nor short,
But tall and of wondrous appearance, the archeress Artemis
    reared
With Apollo; and Ares comes amongst them romping besides
With the keen-eyed Slayer of Argos. But Phoibos Apollo plays,
Stepping fine and high, on the lyre; about him radiance
    shines,   202

And sparklings flash from his feet and tunic of beautiful
    weave.
Leto with tresses of gold and wise Zeus in their great hearts
Feel joy, as they watch their son sport amongst the immortal
    gods.
    How shall I sing a hymn of you, whom hymns have in
      every way praised?
Am I to sing of you surrounded by brides and love,
And tell how you once went wooing Azan's maiden child
Together with godlike Iskhys, Elatos' horse-rich son?
How you went together with Phorbas, son of Triops by birth?
With Erekhtheus? Or with Leukippos, and to Leukippos'
    spouse

   .   .   .   .

On foot, on a car the other; yet he was Triops' match.   213
Or am I to sing how first you traversed the earth to find
An oracular shrine for humans, Apollo who shoot from afar?
When you descended Olympos, you reached Pieria first;
Passed by sandy Lektos, the Ainienes too,
And amidst the Perrhaiboi folk; to Iolkos quickly came,
And onto Kenaion stepped of Euboia famed for ships.
On the plain of Lelantos you stood, but it did not please your
    heart
To set up upon this site your shrine and wooded groves.
Crossing from there the Euripos, Apollo who shoot from afar,
You climbed a holy, green mountain; but from it quickly
    reached   223
Mykalessos, then Teumessos bedded with grassy meads,
And arrived at the seat of Thebes that was covered over with
    trees—
For no one yet of mortals was dwelling in sacred Thebes,
Nor yet did there then exist any tracks or paths across
The wheat-bearing plain of Thebes, but forest held all in its
    grasp.
    From there you went on further, Apollo who shoot from
      afar,
And to Onkhestos came, Poseidon's splendid grove.
There the new-tamed colt draws breath in his distress

At pulling the beautiful chariot; down from his place to the
    earth
The driver, though skilful, leaps and walks along the road; 233
Then for a time the horses rattle the empty car,
Sending dominion away. But if the chariot breaks
Within the wooded grove, they tend to the horses, but lean
And leave the vehicle be—for so from the first was the rite.
To the lord they pray, and the doom of god then guards the
    car.
    From there you went on further, Apollo who shoot from
      afar,
And then arrived at Kephisos, that river whose flowing is fair,
Who from Lilaia pours his water in fair-flowing streams.
Crossing, you reached the town that many a tower protects,
Okalea, Far-worker; came to lush Haliartos next, 243
And went on toward Telphousa. There it pleased your heart
To set up in that tranquil place your shrine and wooded
    groves.
Close beside her you stood, and to her spoke these words:
    'In this place, Telphousa, I plan to set up a beautiful
      shrine
As an oracle sought by humans. Whether they're folk who live
On fertile Peloponnesos, or in Europa dwell
And on isles that waters flow round, they'll always bring to me
    here
Their perfect hundredfold offerings, hoping to hear my
    response.
I'll give all unerring counsel, responding within my rich shrine.'
    When he had in this way spoken, Phoibos Apollo laid 254
Wide and long foundations stretching without a break;
But by this sight Telphousa was angered at heart, and said:
    'Lord Phoibos who work from afar, let me put in your
      mind a thought,
Since in this place it is your plan to set up a beautiful shrine
As an oracle sought by humans, who'll always bring to you
    here
Their perfect hundredfold offerings; ponder my words in your
    mind.

Quick horses' clatter, and mules being watered from my
    sacred springs,
Will always be causing you pain—a human will then more
    wish
To view the well-made cars and the clatter of quick-footed
    steeds,
Than he will your great shrine and the treasures lying heaped
    up inside.   266
But if you would heed me at all—more powerful, lord, and
    brave
You are, of course, than I, and have the greatest strength—
Make your shrine in Krisa, down in Parnassos' fold.
About your well-built altar there will in that place be
No beautiful chariots' jolting or clatter of quick-footed steeds.
The glorious tribes of humans would rather be bringing their
    gifts
To you, Ie-Paieon, and joyful at heart you'd take
The beautiful offerings made by humans who dwell round
    about.'
      So she spoke, and persuaded the Far-shooter's mind, so
      that she herself,
Telphousa, might have—and not the Far-shooter—fame upon
    earth.   276
From there you went on further, Apollo who shoot from afar,
And came to the city peopled by Phlegyai, violent men,
Who, paying no heed to Zeus, used to make their home on
    earth
In a beautiful valley lying near the Kephisian lake.
Rushing on swiftly from there, you approached a mountain
    ridge,
And under snowy Parnassos came to Krisa then,
A slope that faces Zephyr. Above it hangs a crag;
A hollow and rugged valley runs below. This spot
Lord Phoibos Apollo marked out as his lovely shrine's site,
    and said:
      'In this place it is my plan to set up a beautiful shrine 287
As an oracle sought by humans. Whether they're folk who live
On fertile Peloponnesos, or in Europa dwell

And on isles that waters flow round, they'll always bring to me
    here
Their perfect hundredfold offerings, hoping to hear my
    response.
I'll give all unerring counsel, responding within my rich
    shrine.'
    When he had in this way spoken, Phoibos Apollo laid
Wide and long foundations stretching without a break;
Upon them a threshold of stone was placed by Erginos' sons,
Trophonios and Agamedes, dear to the deathless gods;
And countless tribes of humans, using finished blocks,   299
Raised about it a shrine to be famed for ever in song.
    But there was near by a fair-flowing spring, and here the
      Snake
Was slain by the lord son of Zeus with a shot from his mighty
    bow,
Well-fattened and huge though she was, a savage monster,
    who caused
Much harm to humans on earth—much harm to humans
    themselves,
And much to their slender-legged flocks, since she was a
    blood-spattered bane.
From Hera whose throne is golden she once had taken and
    reared
The dread and fierce Typhaon, a bane to mortal men.
Hera had given him birth in anger at Father Zeus,
When Kronos' son had begotten renowned Athena within   309
His head. At once with anger was queenly Hera filled,
And she amongst the immortals gathered together said:
    'All you gods and goddesses, listen how Zeus who gathers
      the clouds
Has begun unprovoked to slight me! He made me his true-
    hearted wife,
And now without me has given bright-eyed Athena birth—
Amongst all the blessed immortals she is beyond compare.
But the runt of all the gods is that son whom I bore myself,
Hephaistos with shrivelled feet. I flung him from my grasp
Into the sea's expanse, but he was welcomed there

By Thetis whose feet are silver, the daughter whom Nereus
    begot,   319
And she brought him amongst her sisters—I wish she had
    done something else
To please the blessed gods. Relentless, subtle in *Craft*,
What else will you now *think up*? How did you dare alone
Give bright-eyed Athena birth? Couldn't I have given her
    birth?
Even so amongst the immortals who make broad heaven their
    home
She would have been called your own. Take care now lest I
    think up
Some wicked plan in future—in fact I'll now contrive
How a son of mine may be born who would be beyond
    compare
Amongst the immortal gods. I'll not bring any disgrace
On your sacred bed or mine, nor shall I be sleeping with
    you,   329
But remote from you I'll be amongst the immortal gods.'
    So she spoke, and far away from the gods she went in her
    wrath.
At once then did cow-eyed, queenly Hera begin to pray,
And with down-turned palm she smote the ground and spoke
    these words:
    'Now listen, Earth, to me, and also broad Heaven above,
And you Titan gods who about great Tartaros dwell
    underground,
From whom come men and gods; let all of you hear me now,
And give me a son without Zeus who'll be no less strong than
    he—
So much mightier let him be as than Kronos was far-seeing
    Zeus.'
    In this way she spoke, and lashed the ground with a
    sturdy hand.   340
The Earth that bears life's nurture was stirred into motion; the
    sight
Gave her joy at heart, for she knew that her wish would be
    fulfilled.

From this moment onward then, till the year had brought its
     end,
She neither at any time came to the bed of Craft-filled Zeus,
Nor did she at any time sit on her richly wrought chair as
     before,
And devise for him shrewd counsels; she stayed in her prayer-
     filled shrines,
Did cow-eyed, queenly Hera, and took from her offerings joy.
But when the months and days were drawing near their end—
The year in its cycle revolving again—and the seasons
     advanced,
She bore then one who was like neither gods nor mortal
     men,   351
The dread and fierce Typhaon, a bane to mortal men.
Then cow-eyed, queenly Hera took and gave him at once
To the Snake, who made him welcome, an evil in evil hands.
To the glorious tribes of humans he used to cause much
     harm,
While the day of doom used to carry whoever met her away—
Until lord Apollo who works from afar let fly at her
His mighty shaft, and she, being racked with cruel pains,
Was lying, loudly gasping, writhing upon the ground.
An unearthly clamour arose beyond words, as she twisted now
     here,
Now there through the wood, and expiring departed her
     bloody life.   361
Then over her in triumph Phoibos Apollo cried:
    'In this place now let you rot on the soil that nurtures
     men.
You won't be an evil affliction to living mortals who eat
The fruit of the bountiful Earth and will to this place bring
Their perfect hundredfold offerings. Neither Typhoeus will
     ward
Grim death from you, nor even Khimaira of hateful name,
But black Earth will make you rot, as will beaming Hyperion's
     rays.'
    He spoke these words in triumph, and darkness covered
     her eyes.

There she was made to rot by the sacred might of the Sun;
And this is the reason why *Pytho* is called by its present
    name,   372
And they title the lord *Pytheios*, because in that place there
The might of the piercing Sun had *rotted* the monster away.
    And then did Phoibos Apollo see that the fair-flowing
        spring
Had deceived him; in anger he made for Telphousa, and soon
        arrived.
Close beside her he stood, and to her spoke these words:
    'Telphousa, you were not destined to keep this lovely spot
By deceiving my mind, and pour forth your fair-flowing water:
        here
Will my fame also be, and not just yours alone.'
    When he had spoken these words, lord Apollo who works
        from afar
Upon her piled a peak with a falling shower of stones.   383
Hiding her streams from view, within the wooded grove
He built for himself an altar close to the fair-flowing spring;
And under the title *Telphousios* all there pray to the lord,
Because he there disfigured sacred Telphousa's streams.
    And then did Phoibos Apollo begin to ponder at heart
What folk he might bring to serve him in rocky Pytho as
        priests.
While revolving this matter he saw a swift ship on the wine-
        dark sea;
Aboard her from Minos' Knossos were many fine Cretan
        men—
It is they who offer the lord his sacrifice, they who report
The decrees of Phoibos Apollo whose sword is of gold, when
        he speaks   395
From the bay-tree proclaiming his oracles down in Parnassos'
        glens.
On a voyage of business and profit toward sandy Pylos town
And its native Pylian race their black ship's course was bound.
But Phoibos Apollo met them; in shape like a dolphin he leaped
Upon their swift ship and lay, a huge dread monster, on
        board.

And if amongst the Cretans any was minded to act,
He shook him in every direction and rattled the planks of the
  ship.
Silent and fearful they sat; throughout the hollow black ship
They were not untying the rigging, nor were they striking the
  sail
Of the ship with dark-coloured prow, but as they had set it in
  place   407
At the outset with oxhide ropes, so onward they held their
  course,
And a southerly gale blew up that roused the swift ship from
  behind.
They first passed Maleia and came along the Lakonian coast
To a city crowned by the sea and a place that belongs to the Sun
Who brings pleasure to mortals—Tainaros. There are the
  thick-fleeced flocks
Of the lordly Sun ever grazing; he owns this pleasant spot.
And there they wished to drop anchor and when they had
  disembarked
To examine this great wonder and with their eyes to watch
Whether the monster would stay aboard the hollow ship
Or would leap out into the swell of the salt sea teeming with
  fish.   417
But the ship which was finely constructed would not answer
  the helm,
But went on alongside of fertile Peloponnesos; with ease
Lord Apollo who works from afar directed her course with the
  breeze.
To Arene and lovely Argyphea forging onward she came,
To Thryon the ford of Alpheios, to Aipy that well-built place,
Then to sandy Pylos town and its native Pylian race.
She went past Krounoi and Khalkis, past Dyme and Elis'
  bright land,
Where power is held by Epeioi; and as for Pherai she aimed
In joy at Zeus' favouring wind, the sheer mountain of Ithake
  hove
From under the clouds into view, and Doulikhion too was
  seen   429

With Same and wooded Zakynthos. But when she had passed
    beyond
The whole of Peloponnesos, and when the vast gulf that sets
    bounds
To fertile Peloponnesos and stretches toward Krisa appeared,
Then came Zephyr, mighty and clear, in accord with Zeus'
    decree,
In a headlong swoop from the sky, so that with utmost speed
The ship would hurtle across the salty water of sea.
Back then again to face the Dawn and Sun they began
To sail, and the lord son of Zeus, Apollo, led them on.
At Krisa, clear to view, where vines abound, they came
To harbour; the sea-going vessel scraped the sandy beach.   439
Lord Apollo who works from afar then leaped out over the
    side
Like a star in the middle of day—there flew from him many
    sparks,
And radiance shot to heaven. He passed within his shrine
Amidst the precious tripods, kindled there a flame,
Revealing his darting rays, and all Krisa was bathed in light.
The wives and fair-girdled daughters of Krisa's men wailed out
At Phoibos' onrush, for great was the dread that he put in
    each heart.
But he bounded aloft from there to fly at the speed of thought
Back to the ship again in the shape of a fine strong man
Enjoying the prime of his youth, whose locks about broad
    shoulders hung;   450
And speaking aloud to the Cretans addressed them with
    winged words:
    'Who are you, strangers? From where do you sail on the
    liquid ways?
Is it on business you travel, or do you recklessly rove
Across the salt sea like pirates, who wander, staking their lives,
Bringing harm to foreign nations? Why sit in such sorrow, and
    not
Disembark on the shore, or take your black ship's tackle
    down?
This at least is the custom of men who are eaters of bread,

When sick with fatigue they come in their black ship from sea
    to land,
And at once their hearts are seized with a longing to taste
    sweet food.'
    In this way Apollo spoke, and put courage within their
      breasts;   462
And then to him in answer the Cretans' leader said:
    'Stranger—although in truth you haven't about you the
      build
Or the look of mortal folk, but are like the immortal gods—
May health and great joy be yours, and heaven grant blessings
    to you!
Now give me an honest answer, to set my mind at rest:
What country is this, what land? What mortals are native
    here?
With a different route in mind we were sailing across the great
    gulf,
For Pylos bound from Crete—our birthplace, we proudly
    boast.
Now here in our ship we've landed, not of our own accord,
By a journey and ways unintended, though yearning to head
    back home.   472
But to this place has some immortal brought us against our
    will.'
    And then to them in answer Apollo the Far-worker said:
'You strangers who dwelt in times past near Knossos where
    many trees grow,
But who now will never again return to your lovely town,
Fair homes, and darling wives, but here will tend my rich shrine
That is honoured by many humans: I am the son of Zeus,
And my boast is that I am Apollo. Across the great gulf of the
    sea
I've brought you, meaning no harm: no, here you'll tend my
    rich shrine
That all humans hold high in esteem, and you'll know the
    plans of the gods,
Through whose will you'll always be honoured, for ever,
    throughout all time.   485

But now quickly obey my instructions: take the sail down first,
Untying the oxhide ropes; then dragging ashore the swift ship,
Unload your cargo and gear; and building an altar there
On the strand where the sea's surf breaks, upon it kindle a
      flame,
Offer white barley and pray while standing about it close by.
As at first in shape like a *dolphin* I leaped on board your swift
      ship
Amidst the cloud-coloured sea, so to me as *Delphinios* pray;
The altar itself will always be *Delphic* and present to view.
Then prepare for yourselves a meal beside your swift black
      ship,
And pour for the blessed gods who have Olympos as
      home.   498
But when you have banished desire for the honey-sweet savour
      of food,
Come along with me and sing the Ie-Paieon hymn,
Until you have made your way to the place where you'll tend
      my rich shrine.'
    When he had in this way spoken, they heeded his words
      and obeyed.
They took the sail down first, untying the oxhide ropes;
Lowered the mast with the forestays, bringing it home to the
      crutch;
Next disembarked themselves on the strand where the sea's
      surf breaks,
And dragged ashore the swift ship high up on the sandy
      beach,
Drawing long props beside it; and built an altar there
On the strand where the sea's surf breaks, upon it kindled a
      flame,   509
Offered white barley and prayed while standing as bidden
      close by.
They made then a meal for themselves beside their swift black
      ship,
And poured for the blessed gods who have Olympos as home.
But when they had banished desire for drink and for food,
      they set out;

Apollo the lord son of Zeus was leading them on their way,
Holding the lyre in his hands and playing a lovely tune,
Stepping fine and high; behind him the Cretans, stamping
    their feet,
Followed toward Pytho and sang the Ie-Paieon hymn—
A hymn such as those that are sung by Cretans within whose
    breasts
The goddess Muse has placed the honey-sweet sound of
    song.   519
Unwearied, they reached a ridge on foot, and suddenly came
To Parnassos, that lovely spot where the god intended to
    dwell,
Honoured by many humans. Leading them further he showed
His holy shrine and rich temple; the spirit was stirred in their
    breasts.
Putting to him a question, the Cretans' leader said:
    'Since far away from our friends and the land of our
        fathers, Lord,
As it pleased your heart, you've brought us, how are we now
    to live?
Consider this point, we ask you. The land here, though lovely
    indeed,
Neither is fit to yield crops nor offers for pasture sweet grass,
Whereby we might live well and attend to humans' needs.'   530
    The son of Zeus, Apollo, smiled and said to them:
'You senseless humans, you wretched creatures wishing at
    heart
For sorrows, hard toils, and troubles! Your answer I'll give
    you with ease
And put in your minds to think on. Let every last one of you
    grasp
A dagger in his right hand and for ever be slaughtering flocks:
They will be there in abundance, all those that are brought for
    me
By the glorious tribes of humans. Stand guard before my shrine
And welcome the tribes of humans who gather here in search,
Above all, of my guidance; but if there will be a rash word or
    deed,

And outrageous conduct, which is the custom of mortal
   men,   541
Then others you'll have as your masters, for ever forced under
   their yoke.
To you now all has been spoken; keep it safe in your
   thoughts.'
  And so farewell I bid you, Zeus and Leto's son;
But I will call to my mind both you and another song.   546

Hymn 4: To Hermes

Sing of Hermes, Muse, of Zeus and Maia's son,
Who over Kyllene reigns and Arkadia rich in flocks,
The immortals' speedy messenger. Maia gave him birth,
That nymph whose tresses are fair, having joined in love with
    Zeus,
Being worthy of reverence. Shunning the throng of blessed
    gods,
She dwelt in a deep-shaded cave, where Kronos' son used to
    join
With the nymph whose tresses are fair at the milking-time of
    night,
While Hera whose arms are pale in the sweetness of sleep was
    clasped,
And neither immortal gods nor mortal humans knew.
But when to its end was approaching the plan of mighty
    Zeus—   10
And now for Maia in heaven her time's tenth moon had
    come—
The issue was brought into daylight, and what had been done
    was made clear:
It was then that she bore a child who was shifty and cunning
    in mind,
A seeker of plunder, a rustler of cattle, a leader of dreams,
A spy who keeps watch in the night, who lies in ambush at
    gates,
And would soon show glorious works amongst the immortal
    gods.
At dawn he was born, at midday was playing the lyre, and stole
At evening cattle owned by Apollo who shoots from afar,
On the day that queenly Maia bore him, the fourth of the
    month.
    When he leaped from his mother's deathless limbs, he
    did not for long   21
Remain in the sacred winnowing-fan, but jumped up to search
For Apollo's cattle, and over the vaulted cave's threshold he
    went.

He found a tortoise there, and vast good fortune gained:
Hermes it was who made the tortoise a singer first.
At the courtyard gates she met him, grazing in front of the
    house
On the thickly flourishing grass, and moving with waddling
    steps.
The speedy son of Zeus with a laugh at the sight at once said:
    'Already I have a sign of great profit: I make no
    complaint.
Hello there, shapely charmer who beat out time for the
    dance,
You feast's companion who come most welcome to view! But
    where   32
Did you get this beautiful toy, a glittering shell, to put on,
You tortoise who live in the mountains? No matter, into the
    house
I will bring you; no slights will you get from me in return for
    your help,
But you will profit me first. It is better to be at home,
Since harm lies out of doors. You will ward off baneful spells
While you live; if you die, most beautiful then your singing
    would be.'
    In this way he spoke, and raising her up with both of his
    hands
He returned back into the house, the lovely toy in his grasp.
There tossing her up, with a knife of grey iron he scooped out
    the flesh
Of the tortoise that dwelt in the mountains, and like the quick
    passing of thought   43
Through the mind of a care-haunted man, or the whirling of
    gleams from eyes,
No sooner said than done was what glorious Hermes devised.
Cutting reed shafts to measure, he fitted them, piercing the
    back,
Through the shell of the tortoise; about it he stretched with his
    cunning the hide
Of a cow, affixed the arms and fastened the yoke to them
    both,

Then stretched seven cords of sheep's gut to serve as
    harmonious strings.
But when he had finished, he tried with the plectrum string by
    string
The lovely toy that he bore, and beneath his hand it made
An astonishing sound. The god began singing a beautiful song
To the tune, exerting himself impromptu, like youths who at
    feasts   56
Give voice to impudent taunts. Declaring his famous descent,
He sang how Kronos' son Zeus and Maia whose sandals are
    fair
Had been wont to hold converse once in the friendly union of
    love;
He extolled the nymph's servants and splendid abode, the
    tripods throughout
Her home, her numerous cauldrons, but had in the midst of
    his song
Still other desires in mind. He set down the hollow lyre
In the sacred winnowing-fan, and lusting for meat he leaped
Down the peak from the fragrant hall: he was plotting an
    outright trick
In his mind, of the sort that thieves carry out in the time of
    black night.
    As the Sun sank under the ground toward Ocean with
    horses and car,   69
At Pieria's shadowy mountains Hermes in haste arrived,
Where deathless cattle were stabled, owned by the blessed
    gods,
On meadows unspoiled and lovely taking of pasture their fill.
The keen-eyed Slayer of Argos, the son whom Maia bore,
Cut off then fifty cattle, whose lowing was loud, from the
    herd;
Turning aside their steps, he drove them by wandering paths
Through sandy ground, and did not forget his fraudulent craft,
Reversing their hooves, the fore-hooves behind, the hind-
    hooves in front,
While walking backwards himself. But at once at the sands of
    the sea

With withies he plaited sandals beyond the description of
      speech,   80
Beyond the grasp of mind, miraculous works that he made
By mixing tamarisk stalks together with myrtle-like shoots.
Of this freshly sprouting wood together an armful he tied,
And bound to his feet without pain the light sandals with
      leaves still attached.
The glorious Slayer of Argos plucked these, avoiding the walk
From Pieria, as making speed a long journey . . .
      By an old man who toiled at a vineyard where flowers
        bloomed he was seen,
As he sped to the plain through Onkhestos bedded with grassy
      meads.
Glorious Maia's son was the first of the pair to speak:
      'Old man who dig at your plants with shoulders curved
        in a stoop,   90
Wine will be yours in plenty, whenever all these bear fruit.
Although you have seen, be blind; be deaf, although you have
      heard;
And be silent, when you on your part suffer no harm at all.'
      He said no more, but hurried the herd of strong cattle on.
Glorious Hermes drove them through many shadowy peaks,
Valleys resounding with echoes, and plains where flowers
      bloomed.
Of the helpful gloom of godly Night the greater part
Was passing, quickly the Morning when folk begin work drew
      near,
And the daughter of lordly Pallas, Megamedes' son,
Brilliant Selene, the Moon, had newly reached her post,   99
When the mighty son of Zeus beside Alpheios' stream
Drove the broad-browed cattle that Phoibos Apollo owned.
Although unbroken, they came to a high-roofed byre and
      troughs
Before a magnificent meadow. There having on fodder well fed
The cattle whose lowing was loud, and then driven them into
      the byre
In a throng, as they chewed on lotos and galingale moist with
      dew,

He brought many sticks together, and strove for the craft of
     fire.
He seized and stripped with iron a bay-tree's splendid bough

   .   .   .   .   .   .

That was firmly fixed in his grasp, and upwards heat was
     breathed:
Hermes it was who first discovered fire-sticks and fire.   111
Taking many dry logs entire, in abundance he piled them up
In a pit that was sunk in the ground, and a flame began
     shining there
That sent far out a blast of fiercely blazing fire.
While the might of renowned Hephaistos kindled the flames,
     close by
A pair of lowing black heifers Hermes dragged outside;
Possessed of great power, he hurled them both gasping onto
     their backs
To earth, inclined and rolled them, piercing their spines
     straight through,
And followed one task with another, cutting their fat-rich
     meat.
Transfixed on wooden spits he roasted together the flesh,
The chines of honour's share, the black blood crammed in the
     guts.   123
While these on the ground were lying there, on a rugged rock
He stretched out the hides, as still they are now after all this
     time,
A long time since these events, and will unceasingly be.
But then Hermes the joyful at heart drew onto a smooth, flat
     stone
The rich fruits of his labour, divided twelve portions for lots to
     assign,
And added to each in perfection honour's share of chine.
Then glorious Hermes craved the meat of the rite, for the
     scent
Distressed him, immortal though he was, with its sweetness;
     but not
Even so did his bold spirit yield, for all that he yearned to
     thrust

The meat down his sacred throat. He set down in the high-
        roofed byre   134
The fat and the plentiful meat, but at once he raised them
        aloft,
The sign of his youthful theft. Collecting dry sticks, he
        destroyed
The whole feet, the whole heads with the breath of fire. But
        when the god
Had fittingly finished it all, in Alpheios where eddies swirl
        deep
He cast his sandals, quenched the embers, and spent all the
        night
Spreading black ash with sand in Selene's beautiful light.
        To Kyllene's brilliant peaks he quickly came once more
By morning; none of the blessed gods or mortal men
In his long journey's course had met him, and not a dog had
        barked.
The speedy son of Zeus, having turned himself sideways,
        passed   146
Through the chink of the hall-door's lock like a harvest-time
        breeze or a mist.
He went straight on and reached the rich inner shrine of the
        cave,
Moving with soft steps forward—his walk was so silent, it
        seemed
His feet were not touching the ground. In the winnowing-fan
        in haste
Glorious Hermes climbed; around his shoulders he wrapped
The swaddling-bands, and lay like an infant child, having fun
With the sheet that he held at his hams, while keeping
        enclosed on his left
The lovely tortoise-lyre. But the god did not escape
His goddess mother's sight, and she then spoke these words:
        'What are you up to, subtle rogue, arriving here   155
In the night from who knows where, parading your barefaced
        cheek?
It is now my firm belief that with bonds about your ribs
Against which struggle is futile, bonds that nothing can loose,

You will pass out through the porch in the grasp of Leto's son,
Rather than that you will plunder and rob when you please in
        the glens.
Be off back where you came from! In you your father begot
A vast vexation for mortal men and immortal gods.'

        To her in answer Hermes spoke these cunning words:
'Mother, why aim this abuse at me, as if I were
An infant child who knows but a few naughty tricks in his
        mind,   164
A timid babe, whose mother's rebukes make him cower in
        fright?
I shall enter whatever craft is best, so keeping us both
In clover for ever: the two of us will not endure
Staying here in this place, the only immortals deprived of gifts
And prayers, as you are bidding. Better that all one's days
Be spent conversing amongst the immortals with riches, wealth,
And plenty of booty, than sitting at home in a murky cave.
As for honour, I too shall enter that rite which Apollo enjoys.
If my father will not allow me, then I shall try—it is in
My power—to be the leader of thieves; and if the son   176
Of glorious Leto comes in search of me, I think
Something else even worse will happen to him, for I shall go
To Pytho, to break my way inside his great abode.
From there I shall plunder in plenty tripods surpassingly fair,
Cauldrons and gold, and gleaming iron in plenty as well,
And a lot of clothes—and you will see it, if you wish.'

        So they addressed one another, the son of Zeus who bears
The *aigis* and queenly Maia, as Dawn the early-born
Was rising from deep-flowing Ocean, bringing to mortals her
        light.
But Apollo had reached Onkhestos, the lovely, hallowed
        grove   186
Of the loud-roaring Holder of Earth. He found the old man
        there
Grazing a beast, his vineyard's bulwark, beside the road.
Glorious Leto's son was the first of the pair to speak:
        'Old man, you bramble-plucker of grassy Onkhestos
        there,

I've reached this place from Pieria, searching for cattle that
      came—
All of them heifers, all with twisted horns—from my herd.
The black bull was grazing alone away from the rest, and
      behind
Him followed the bright-eyed dogs, like four men with one
      purpose in mind.
These dogs and the bull were left there, and that is a marvel
      indeed;
But the heifers, just as the Sun was setting, went from the
      soft   198
Meadow-field, away from sweet pasture. Tell me, aged one
      born
Long ago, have you seen any man who with them travelled the
      path?'
    The old man, making his answer, addressed him with
      these words:
'My friend, it's a difficult task to tell all you might see with
      your eyes.
Many wayfarers travel the road: intent on much evil are some,
While others have worthy ends, and it's hard to know each
      one.
But I spent the whole day till sunset digging around the ridge
Of the vineyard whose soil yields wine; now I cannot swear to
      it, sir,
But I thought that I saw a child, and this child, whoever he was,
Was following fine-horned heifers, although a mere infant
      babe.   210
He was grasping a stick and walking from side to side, from
      the rear
Of the herd was pressing them back, and was keeping turned
      towards him their heads.'
    The old man spoke; the god, when he heard, advanced
      along
The road with greater speed. He was watching a long-winged
      bird,
And suddenly knew that the thief was the son of Kronos' son
      Zeus.

In haste toward holy Pylos Apollo the lord son of Zeus
Rushed on in his search for the shambling cattle, his broad
      shoulders wrapped
In purple cloud. The Far-shooter noticed the tracks and said:
    'Well now, a mighty marvel is this that I see with my
      eyes!
Those at least are tracks of cattle with upright horns,   220
Yet back to the asphodel meadow they're turned. But these
      are steps
That belong to no man or woman, to no grey wolves or bears
Or lions, nor do I think to some Centaur with shaggy-maned
      neck,
Whoever with swift feet takes such astounding strides as these.
Strange as they are over there, these here are stranger still.'
    Apollo the lord son of Zeus with these words rushed
      onward and came
To Kyllene's wood-clad peak and the deep-shaded lair in the
      rock
Where the heavenly nymph had borne the child of Kronos'
      son Zeus.
A lovely scent was spreading throughout the holy peak,
And upon the grass went grazing many slender-legged
      sheep.   232
Across the threshold of stone and into the murky cave
Quickly then entered the Far-shooter, mighty Apollo himself.
    When Zeus and Maia's son saw Apollo who shoots from
      afar
Raging about his cattle, he snuggled down amidst
The fragrant swaddling-bands: like ash enfolding a pile
Of tree-stump embers, Hermes curled himself up when he
      glimpsed
The god who works from afar. In a small space together he
      pressed
His head, his hands, his feet, like a babe who is fresh from the
      bath
And is summoning pleasant sleep, though wide awake he was,
And kept the tortoise-lyre beneath the pit of his arm.   242
But Zeus and Leto's son knew well without mistake

The beautiful mountain nymph and her son, a child who,
    though small,
Was cloaked in deceitful guile; and peering throughout each
    nook,
With a gleaming key he opened three secret chambers filled
With nektar and lovely ambrosia. Lying inside was gold
And silver in plenty, and plenty of clothes that belonged to the
    nymph
Of crimson and silvery hue, such treasures as sacred abodes
Of blessed gods contain. When Leto's son had explored
The nooks of the spacious abode, to glorious Hermes he said:
    'You child who lie in the winnowing-fan, inform me at
        once   255
Of my cattle, or soon we'll differ, and not in a seemly way.
For into murky Tartaros, into the dreadful doom
Of darkness that none can escape, I'll toss you. You'll not be
    released
By mother or father to see the light again, but beneath
The earth you'll be gone, and will rule amongst the little
    men.'
    To him in answer Hermes spoke these cunning words:
'What's this unfriendly speech, son of Leto? You've come here
    in search
Of cattle whose haunts are the fields? Not a sight did I see,
    not a fact
Did I learn, not a word did I hear from another's lips, I
    could
Not reveal the least information, I could not at all collect   264
An informer's fee. I don't even look like a mighty man
Who rustles cattle, and that is no business of mine—till now
Other matters have been on my mind. What's been on my
    mind is sleep
And the milk of my mother, keeping the swaddling-bands
    wrapped round
My shoulders, and warm bath-water. No one had better find
    out
The cause of this quarrel—it would quite astound the
    immortals to learn

That a new-born babe had passed through his porch with
    cattle whose haunts
Are the fields! But that's an implausible claim you make: I
    was born
Just yesterday, soft are my feet, and rough underfoot is the
    ground.
Yet by my father's head I'll swear, if you wish, a great
    oath: 274
I neither declare myself to be guilty, nor have I seen
Anyone else who stole your cattle, whatever it is
These "cattle" may be—about them this rumour is all that I
    hear.'
    In this way he spoke, and had in his eyes a knowing
      gleam,
As he tossed about with his brows while gazing now here, now
    there,
Giving long whistles, paying the other's words no heed.
To him with gentle laughter Apollo the Far-worker said:
    'My fine, deceitful schemer, it is my firm belief
That during the hours of night you'll often break your way
Inside the well-built home of more than one man alone,   284
And stripping his house without noise you'll force him to
    make the ground
His seat, to judge by your talk! And in glens of the mountain
    you'll vex
Many herdsmen whose haunts are the fields, whenever lusting
    for meat
You encounter herds of cattle and sheep with woolly fleece.
But unless you desire to take your last and final nap,
Get down from the winnowing-fan, companion of gloomy
    night.
For this then indeed will be your share of honour amongst
The immortals: you will for ever be called the Leader of
    Thieves.'
    With these words Phoibos Apollo, to carry him, seized the
      child.
But the mighty Slayer of Argos, while being raised up in his
    hands,   295

Took thought and sent out an omen, the brazen labouring
     man
Of his belly, a wicked messenger, after which quickly he
     sneezed.
Apollo heard it and threw illustrious Hermes to earth,
Seated himself before him, though eager to speed on the way,
Aiming his taunts at Hermes, and to him spoke these words:
    'Take courage, swaddled infant, Zeus and Maia's son.
I shall then indeed discover where my strong cattle are,
By means of these omens—and you, moreover, will lead the
     way.'
    In this way he spoke, but Kyllenian Hermes swiftly
     jumped up,
Moving with haste. With his hands he pushed about both of
     his ears   305
The swaddling-bands entwined around his shoulders, and
     said:
    'Where are you bearing me, Far-worker, fiercest of all the
     gods?
Is it anger over your cattle that makes you annoy me like this?
May the race of cattle perish! For I stole no cattle of yours,
Nor have I seen any other who stole them, whatever it is
That "cattle" may be—about them this rumour is all that I
     hear.
But pay and receive satisfaction with Kronos' son Zeus as the
     judge.'
    But when the shepherd Hermes and Leto's splendid son
Had explored all these points in detail, their minds on
     different ends—
Apollo, speaking unerringly, not without justice desired   316
To lay hands on glorious Hermes because of his cattle, while
     he,
The Kyllenian, wanted to dupe with tricks and with cunning
     words
The God of the Silver Bow—but when Hermes, for all his
     wiles,
Found him well able to cope, then quickly he walked through
     the sand

In front, and behind him followed Zeus and Leto's son.
On the summit of fragrant Olympos the beautiful children of
      Zeus
Came at once to their father, Kronos' son, since there for them
      both
The scales of justice lay waiting . . . held snowy Olympos,
And the deathless immortals were gathering after golden-
      throned Dawn.
With Hermes stood Apollo, God of the Silver Bow,   327
In front of the knees of Zeus; and Zeus who thunders on high
Questioned his brilliant son, and to him spoke these words:
    'Phoibos, from where have you rustled this pleasing
      plunder, a babe
Who's just been born, who has about him a herald's look?
A serious matter is this that's come to the council of gods!'
    The lord Apollo who works from afar addressed him in
      turn:
'Father, no trifling tale will you be hearing soon,
Although it is your taunt that I am the only one
Who has a liking for plunder. I found a certain child—
This outright brigand here—amongst Kyllene's peaks,   337
When I'd crossed a vast tract of land. An impudent rogue he is,
And never have I, at least, seen any who'd be his match,
Of gods or those men who swindle mortals over the earth.
He stole from their meadow my cattle, at evening he drove
      them away
By the shore where waves were crashing, and straight for Pylos
      he aimed.
And the tracks were twofold, prodigious, fit to marvel at,
And a marvellous deity's work. For while the black dust
      displayed,
Turned back to the asphodel meadow, prints that those cattle
      made,
This impossible beggar himself was crossing the sandy ground
Neither on feet nor hands, but by means of some other
      scheme   348
He left an astounding trail, as though walking on saplings of
      oak.

So long as he sped over sand, all the tracks were distinct in
    the dust;
But when he had passed beyond the great path that led
    through the sand,
The cattle's trail and his own soon vanished upon the hard
    ground—
Though a mortal man perceived him driving toward Pylos the
    herd
Of cattle whose brows are broad. But when he had shut them
    away
To rest in quiet repose, and hurtled then hotfoot along
From this side to that of the road, he lay down in the
    winnowing-fan,
Looking like gloomy night, in a murky cave's deep shade,
Where he could not be reached by even an eagle's piercing
    gaze.   360
And he gave his eyes a good rub with his hands, as he busied
    himself
With deceit, then without more ado he uttered in forthright
    terms
This speech: "Not a sight did I see, not a fact did I learn, not
    a word
Did I hear from another's lips, I could not reveal the least
Information, I could not at all collect an informer's fee.'"
    When he had in this way spoken, Phoibos Apollo sat
      down;
But Hermes in turn replying spoke from the other side,
And pointed at Kronos' son, the master of all the gods:
    'Father Zeus, to you of course I'll tell the truth,
For I am honest, and don't know how to tell a lie.   369
In search of shambling cattle he came to our house today,
Just as the Sun was rising, and brought no blessed gods
As witnesses or observers. Many a threat he made
That he would in broad Tartaros hurl me, since his is the
    tender bloom
Of youth that loves renown, while I was but yesterday born—
He himself is aware of these facts—and have not at all the look
Of a mighty man who rustles cattle. Believe me, since you

Proclaim yourself my father. May I be blessed so sure
As I drove no cattle home, nor over the threshold went—
And I'm telling the perfect truth. I have great respect for the
      Sun   381
And other deities; you I love and him I dread.
That I am not guilty you are yourself aware, but I'll give
A mighty oath besides: I am not, by this well-adorned
Front door of immortals! Some day I'll pay him back for his
      harsh
Inquisition, strong though he be; let you give the younger
      your help.'
    The Kyllenian Slayer of Argos winked as he uttered these
      words,
And he kept without casting aside the swaddling-bands on his
      arm.
Loud was the laughter of Zeus when he saw the roguish child
Denying about the cattle in fine and skilful speech.
But he ordered them both to make search, at one with each
      other in mind,   391
And instructed Conductor Hermes to lead the way and
      reveal—
Without any mischievous plots—where he had the strong
      cattle concealed.
The son of Kronos nodded, and splendid Hermes obeyed,
Persuaded with ease by the mind of *aigis*-bearing Zeus.
    Rushing toward sandy Pylos, these beautiful children of
      Zeus
Both came to Alpheios' ford, to the fields and high-roofed byre
Where during the hours of night the livestock were given their
      feed.
There, while Hermes then passed inside the cave of stone,
And began to drive out the strong cattle into the light of day,
The son of Leto, glancing aside, observed the hides   403
Upon the steep rock, and of glorious Hermes was quick to
      inquire:
    'How were you able, you trickster, to flay two heifers'
      hides,
Although you're just a new-born infant child? I'm amazed

Myself at what in future that strength of yours will be—
Kyllenian, son of Maia, you must not grow up tall.'

    He spoke these words and started to wind with his hands
      strong bonds
Of withy about him; but these beneath his feet in the earth
Upon that selfsame spot took root at once, like grafts
Entwining one with another, and spreading with ease over all
The cattle whose haunts were the fields through deceitful
      Hermes' will,   413
While Apollo looked on with wonder. Then sidelong his gaze
      at the ground
The mighty Slayer of Argos aimed, being eager therein
To hide the gleaming fire; but he soothed with perfect ease—
Strong though he was—the Far-shooter, glorious Leto's son,
In accord with his own desire. He tried with the plectrum
      string
By string the lyre, which he took on his left; beneath his hand
It made an astonishing sound, and Phoibos Apollo laughed
For joy. The lovely burst of heavenly music passed
Through his mind, and while he listened sweet longing seized
      him at heart.
But Maia's son, while playing to lovely effect on the lyre,   423
Took courage and stood on the left of Phoibos Apollo; at once,
As he played the clear notes, he started in prelude to sing—
      and the sound
Of his voice was lovely—bringing to pass the immortal gods
And shadowy Earth in his song, recounting how first they
      were born,
And how each obtained his share. Of the gods he first honoured
      in song
Mnemosyne mother of Muses, for she was assigned Maia's
      son;
To the other immortal gods the splendid son of Zeus
Gave honour according to age and as they each were born,
Telling all in a seemly way, while playing the lyre on his arm.
Love that he could not resist took hold of Apollo at heart,   434
And he in speech to Hermes gave voice to winged words:

    'Slayer of Cattle, Contriver, Performer of Toil, you Feast's

Companion, fifty heifers is your invention's worth!
I think then indeed in our quarrel we'll part from each other
    in peace.
But now come, tell me this, you shifty son of Maia, from birth
Did you have these miraculous skills, or was there one
    amongst
The immortals or mortal men who gave you the marvellous
    gift
And revealed to you heavenly song? For with wonder my ears
    are filled
At this sound for the first time uttered that never has yet, I
    declare,
Been learnt by men or immortals who dwell in Olympian
    homes,   445
Except by you, you robber, Zeus and Maia's son!
What is the craft, the music of sorrows that none can resist,
The beaten track? For truly can merriment, love, sweet sleep
Be gained all three together. I serve the Muses who dwell
On Olympos, whose joy is in dancing, the splendid path of
    song,
Melody's sprightly strains, the delightful wailing of flutes;
But not yet have I felt in my mind such joy as this at aught
    else,
Of all those dextrous skills that the young display at feasts—
I'm amazed, son of Zeus, how lovely these tunes that you're
    playing sound.
But now since, despite being small, you have knowledge of
    glorious schemes,   456
Sit, my fine fellow, and praise your elders at heart. For now
Renown will be yours and your mother's amongst the
    immortal gods—
And this is the truth that I'll tell you, yes, by this cornelwood
    spear!—
I'll seat you in glory and wealth amongst the immortals as
    Guide,
I'll give you splendid gifts, and I'll not play you false in the
    end.'

    To him in answer Hermes spoke these cunning words:

'You take great care in asking me, god who works from afar;
Yet I don't grudge at all that you enter this craft of mine—
You'll know it this very day. I want to be kindly to you
In counsel and speech—but you know everything well in your
    mind.   467
For you, son of Zeus, are the first amongst the immortals to
    sit,
Being so noble and strong; sagacious Zeus with all
Due reverence loves you, to you he has granted splendid gifts
And honours. They say you've learnt prophecies, Far-worker,
    spoken by Zeus—
From Zeus come all things decreed. Now in these I've learnt
    myself
That you, my boy, are rich—but you can freely choose
To learn whatever you wish. Well, since your heart is set
On playing the lyre, make melody, play, and busy yourself
With splendid celebration, receiving the lyre from me—
But furnish me, friend, with renown. Produce melodious
    tunes,   478
As you hold in your hands your clear-voiced companion,
    expert in speech
That is fair and fine and seemly. Bring it then at your ease
To the bounteous feast, the delightful dance, the revel that
    loves
Renown, a source of merriment by both night and day.
When one who has learned the knowledge puts to it questions
    with craft
And wisdom, it cries out and teaches joys of all sorts that charm
The mind, being easily played with a gently familiar touch,
Escaping painful exertion; but when at the outset one
Who lacks knowledge puts to it questions with violence, then
    it will yield
A pointless, high-pitched jangle—but you can freely choose   489
To learn whatever you wish. Now I shall grant you this,
You splendid young fellow of Zeus, but let us then, Far-
    worker, graze
The cattle whose haunts are the fields on the pastures of
    mountain and plain

That gives nurture to horses. The heifers will then be mated
    with bulls,
And will bear in abundance together calves both female and
    male—
But you must not grow fiercely angry, despite your greed for
    gain!'
    With these words he proffered the lyre. Apollo, accepting
    the gift,
Put in Hermes' palm the gleaming whip that he held, and
    bestowed
Upon him the tending of herds of cattle; Maia's son
Accepted these gifts with joy. Then Leto's splendid son,   500
Lord Apollo the Far-worker, tried with the plectrum string by
    string
The lyre, which he took on his left; beneath his hand it made
An astonishing sound, and the god sang a beautiful song to
    the tune.
    When the two of them then had turned toward the divine
    meadow-field
The cattle, they themselves, the beautiful children of Zeus,
Rushed back to snowy Olympos, taking delight in the lyre;
Sagacious Zeus rejoiced, and brought them together as friends.
Hermes without reserve felt love for Leto's son—
As still he does even now—when for a token he put
The lovely lyre in the palm of the god who shoots from
    afar,
        509
And he, having learnt, began to play it upon his arm.
But Hermes sought out for himself the craft of another skill:
He made the syrinx' piping that can far away be heard.
And then the son of Leto to Hermes spoke these words:
    'I'm afraid, son of Zeus, Conductor, subtle in guile, that
    you'll steal
The lyre back and my curving bow. For you hold the honour
    from Zeus
Of founding acts of barter for humans all over the earth
That gives to many their nurture. But if you could bring
    yourself
To swear the gods' great oath, by either nodding your head

Or making your vow upon the potent water of Styx,   519
You would accomplish everything pleasing and dear to my
    heart.'
    And then the son of Maia promised with downward nod
Never to steal away whatever the Far-shooter owned,
Or approach his solid abode. In turn with downward nod,
To mark their alliance and love, Apollo, Leto's son,
Declared that amongst the immortals no other would be more
    dear,
Neither god nor man begotten by Zeus. And out a perfect
   .   .   .   .

Amongst immortals and humans I'll make a sign which I trust
And honour at heart. But I'll give you besides a beautiful rod
Of fortune and riches, golden and branching in three;
    unscathed   530
It will keep you while bringing to pass all decrees of words
    and of deeds
That are good, all those that I claim to have learnt from the
    voice of Zeus.
But prophecy, splendid fellow, about which you ask without
    end,
It's decreed that neither yourself nor another immortal may
    learn.
For this is a matter known to the mind of Zeus, while I
In pledge have nodded down and sworn a mighty oath
That I alone of the gods who live for ever shall know
The shrewd-minded counsel of Zeus; and let you not
    command,
Brother with rod of gold, that I disclose the decrees
That far-seeing Zeus devises. Of humans one I'll harm   541
And profit another, while many times around I herd
The tribes of unenvied humans. My voice will profit him
Whose coming is guided by speech and flights of birds that
    bring
Fulfilment—my voice will profit him, and I shall not
Deceive him. But he who trusts in birds of idle talk,
Who wants to inquire of our prophecy more than reason
    permits

And have more knowledge than gods who always exist, I say
His journey will be in vain—though I would accept his gifts.
But there's something else that I'll tell you, glorious Maia's
    son
By *aigis*-bearing Zeus, the immortals' speedy god.   551
For certain holy virgins, sisters by birth, there are,
Who all three exult in quick wings. They have white barley
    bestrewn
On their heads, and inhabit dwellings down in Parnassos' fold,
Teachers far-off of a prophecy practised by me when still
A boy with the cattle I was, and my father paid no heed.
Flying in one way now, and now in another, from there,
They feed on combs of honey and bring all things to pass.
And when they are inspired from eating pale honey, they wish
To speak truth of their own free will; but if deprived of the
    gods'
Sweet food, they quiver then amongst one another and lie.   563
These then I grant you: by making exact inquiry delight
Your own mind; should you teach a mortal man, he'll often
    hear
Your voice, if he's lucky. Possess, son of Maia, these gifts, and
    take care
Of black cattle whose haunts are the fields, of horses and
    hard-working mules

   .   .   .   .

And that over bright-eyed lions and boars whose tusks are
    white,
And that over dogs and flocks, as many as broad Earth
    rears,
And that over all cattle glorious Hermes hold sway, and
    alone
The appointed messenger be to Hades, who, though he gives
No gifts, will yet of honour give not the smallest share.
    In this way the lord Apollo showed love for Maia's
    son
                               574
With friendship of every sort, and the son of Kronos bestowed
Favour upon him besides. With all mortals and immortals
    both

He has dealings; seldom though does he help, but unceasingly
    cheats
Throughout the gloomy night the tribes of mortal men.
    And so farewell I bid you, Zeus and Maia's son;
But I will call to my mind both you and another song.   580

HYMN 5: TO APHRODITE

Speak to me, Muse, of golden Aphrodite's works,
The Cyprian's—she who sends sweet desire on the gods, and
    subdues
The tribes of mortal men, the birds that fly through the air,
And all the many wild beasts that are nurtured by land and
    sea:
The works of Kythera's fair-crowned goddess concern all these.
    There are three whose minds she cannot persuade or
    beguile—and the child
Of Zeus who bears the *aigis*, bright-eyed Athena, is one.
For not pleasing to her are golden Aphrodite's works,
But what is pleasing to her are wars and Ares' work,
Combats and battles, and being busy with splendid
    works—   11
She was the first who taught the craftsmen on earth to make
    carts
And chariots gleaming with bronze, and she taught her
    splendid works
To the soft-skinned maidens in halls, inspiring each one's
    mind.
    Aphrodite the lover of smiles can also never subdue
Artemis—goddess with distaff of gold, whose cry resounds—
In love: for what is pleasing to her is the bow and to kill
The beasts on the mountains, lyres and dances, piercing cries,
Shaded groves, and the city belonging to righteous men.
    Aphrodite's works fail to please the revered maid Hestia
    too,
Whom Kronos the cunning of mind begot as his first-born
    child,   22
But then as his youngest he gave her a second birth, through
    the will
Of Zeus who bears the *aigis*, his queenly goddess child
Whom Poseidon wooed and Apollo. But she, unwilling to wed,
Firmly rejected her suitors, and swore a mighty oath
(Which has been brought to fulfilment), when by his head she
    had grasped

Father Zeus who bears the *aigis*, a virgin to be for all time,
Brilliant amongst the goddesses. Father Zeus then gave
A beautiful share of honour to her in marriage's place,
And taking the choicest portion she sat in the midst of the
      house.
She is a holder of honour in all the shrines of the gods,   31
And by all mortals is counted the eldest amongst the gods.
     The minds of these three she cannot persuade or beguile;
      none else
Can escape Aphrodite, of blessed gods or mortal men.
She even misled the wits of Zeus whom thunder delights,
Who has the greatest power, of honour the greatest share:
Deceiving even his shrewd mind whenever she wished,
She easily joined him together with mortal women in love,
Having made him forgetful of Hera, his sister and wife, who is
Of all the immortal goddesses much the fairest in form—
The most glorious daughter that Kronos the cunning of mind
      begot   42
With Mother Rhea, and Zeus who knows unperishing schemes
Caused her then to become his revered and true-hearted wife.
     But Zeus put the sweet desire even in Aphrodite's heart
That she be joined together in love with a mortal man,
To ensure with the utmost speed that she herself might be
To a mortal's bed no stranger, nor ever be making the boast
Amidst the gods' assembly, laughing sweetly, that she,
Aphrodite the lover of smiles, had joined together the gods
With mortal women who bore to immortals mortal sons,
And that she had the goddesses joined in love with mortal
      men.   52
So Zeus put sweet desire for Ankhises within her heart:
On the lofty peaks of Ida where many fountains flow
He was grazing cattle then, and was like the immortals in build.
     Aphrodite the lover of smiles, when once she set eyes on
      him,
Was filled with yearning; desire completely conquered her
      mind.
She went to the island of Cyprus, and entered her fragrant
      shrine

At Paphos, the place where her precinct and fragrant altar are
 found;
There, having gone inside, she closed the gleaming doors.
And there the Graces washed her, anointed her there with oil,
With the deathless oil that covers the gods who always
 exist,   62
Heavenly, sweet-smelling oil which had been perfumed for
 her.
And when she had clothed herself well with fair robes all
 about her flesh,
And was decked with golden adornments, on toward Troy
 then rushed
Aphrodite the lover of smiles, leaving fragrant Cyprus behind,
Completing the journey at speed high up amongst the clouds.
  To Ida, where many fountains flow, the mother of beasts,
She came, and over the mountain straight for the farmstead
 she aimed.
Grey wolves and bright-eyed lions fawning behind her went,
Bears and swift-moving panthers never sated with deer.
Delighted at heart by the sight, she put in their breasts
 desire,   73
And all together they mated in pairs through the shadowy
 vales.
But she herself arrived at the finely constructed huts,
And found left behind at the farmstead, alone, apart from the
 rest,
Ankhises, the hero possessed of beauty derived from the gods.
While over the grassy pastures the others all followed the herd,
He, left behind at the farmstead, alone, apart from the rest,
Was strolling now this way, now that, and was piercingly
 playing the lyre.
But then before him stood Aphrodite daughter of Zeus,
And in stature and form she resembled a maiden as yet
 untamed,
So that when with his eyes he perceived her he would not
 succumb to dread.   83
Ankhises, on seeing, took note, and was struck with awe at her
 form,

Her stature, her glossy clothes. For she had put on a robe
That blazed more brightly than fire, and was wearing twisted
        whorls
And gleaming floweret-cups; and chains surpassingly fair
About her tender neck were hanging, beautiful, gold,
Of exquisite craft right through—it seemed as though the
        moon
About her tender breasts were shining, a marvel to view.
Ankhises was seized with passion, and to her spoke these
        words:

    'You are welcome, Queen, to this house, whoever you are
        of the Blest,
Whether Artemis, Leto, golden Aphrodite perhaps,   93
Themis of noble birth, or Athena whose eyes are bright.
Or you that have come here perhaps are one of the Graces,
        who serve
As companions to all of the gods, and are called immortals
        themselves;
Or else you're one of the nymphs who inhabit beautiful
        groves,
Or one of the nymphs who make this beautiful mountain their
        home,
And the springs whence rivers flow, and the meadows where
        grasses grow.
On a summit seen from all sides I'll build an altar for you,
And in every season I'll make you beautiful offerings there;
But let you have a kindly heart, and grant that I be a man
Of distinction amongst the Trojans; offspring blooming with
        health   104
Bestow in future on me, and permit me to lead myself
A long and happy life, to see the light of the Sun
With blessings amongst my people, and reach the threshold of
        age.'

    To him then in answer spoke Aphrodite daughter of
        Zeus:
'Ankhises, greatest in glory of humans born on earth,
I am no god. Why think that I'm like the immortals? No,
I'm just a mortal, a woman the mother that gave me birth.

My father is Otreus, whose name is renowned—you've heard
       it, perhaps—
Who over the whole of strongly fortified Phrygia rules.
But I have perfect knowledge of your people's language and
       ours.   113
For the nurse who reared me at home was a Trojan; right
       from the first
She received me, a tiny babe, from the hands of my mother,
       to tend;
And that's how I've also good knowledge of your people's
       language, at least.
But now the Slayer of Argos who bears the rod of gold
From the dance of Artemis, goddess with distaff of gold,
       whose cry
Resounds, has snatched me away. We were playing, many
       nymphs
And cattle-yielding maidens, ringed by a measureless throng;
But then the Slayer of Argos who bears the rod of gold
Snatched me and carried me over the many worked fields of
       men,
And over a vast expanse of land unallotted, untilled,   123
Where wander through shadowy vales wild beasts that eat raw
       flesh,
And I thought that I wouldn't touch the grain-growing earth
       with my feet.
But the god said that I would be called Ankhises' wedded
       wife,
Who would lie in your bed and give birth to splendid children
       for you.
The mighty Slayer of Argos pointed and showed me the way,
And then departed amongst the tribes of immortals once more;
But here to you I came, and upon me was mighty constraint.
But I beg you, by Zeus and your parents—and they, I think,
       must be
Worthy folk, for none who are base could beget such a man—
Take me now and show me, untamed and untried in love,   133
To your father and true-hearted mother, your brothers who
       share your blood:

They'll find me not an unfit, but a suitable daughter-in-law.
But send a messenger quickly to Phrygia's swift-mounted folk,
To tell my father the news, and my mother, who'll now be
    distressed.
To you they'll send an abundance of gold and of woven garb,
And let you accept as payment their many and splendid gifts.
When you have done all this, prepare then to hold the feast
Of desirable marriage, which men and immortal gods esteem.'
    When so she had spoken, the goddess put sweet desire in
    his heart.
Ankhises was seized with passion; he spoke, and addressed her
    aloud: 144
    'If a mortal is what you are, and a woman gave you birth,
If Otreus is, as you say, your father whose name is renowned,
If the will of the deathless Conductor, of Hermes, has brought
    you here,
If you'll always be called my wife, then of gods and mortal
    men
There's none who'll stop me from joining in love with you
    right now—
Not even Apollo the Far-shooter launching arrows of woe
From his silver bow. I'd be willing, Lady with goddesses'
    looks,
Having once climbed into your bed, to enter Hades' abode.'
    With these words he took her hand; Aphrodite the lover
    of smiles
Turned herself round and walked, her beautiful eyes cast
    down,   156
To the bed that was finely strewn in the place where for the
    lord
It had already with blankets been softly spread—but on top
Were lying the skins of bears and of lions with deep-throated
    roar,
Beasts that upon the high mountains the hero himself had
    slain.
And when the pair climbed into the finely constructed bed,
Ankhises first took from her flesh the gleaming adornments
    she wore,

The brooches and twisted whorls, the floweret-cups and
    chains;
He loosed her girdle next, slipped off her glossy clothes,
And laid them down on a chair that was studded with silver
    nails.
By the gods' will then and fate he lay, a mortal man,   167
Beside an immortal goddess, and knew not what he did.
    But as the time approached when herdsmen drive back to
      the byre
Their cattle and flocks of fat sheep from the pastures where
    flowers bloom,
Then on Ankhises she poured a pleasant draught of sweet
    sleep,
And put on her beautiful clothes. In all her fine attire,
Brilliant amongst the goddesses, there in the hut she stood:
Her head reached the well-wrought roof-beam, and deathless
    beauty shone
From her cheeks, such as to Kythera's fair-crowned goddess
    belongs.
Waking him up from slumber, she spoke, and addressed him
    aloud:
    'Stir yourself, son of Dardanos. Why this unwaking
      sleep?   177
Consider now if the same as when first you saw me I seem.'
    In this way she spoke, and he from slumber heard her at
      once.
As soon as he saw Aphrodite's neck and beautiful eyes,
He felt his heart stricken with dread, and turned his gaze
    aside.
Back down again he sank, and with a blanket hid
His handsome face. In plea he addressed her with winged
    words:
    'From that very moment, goddess, when first I set eyes on
      you,
I knew that you were divine; but you didn't tell me the truth.
Yet by Zeus who bears the *aigis* I beg you, don't let me dwell
Amongst humans in strengthless existence, but show me your
    mercy—the man   189

Who sleeps with deathless goddesses has no flourishing life.'
    To him then in answer spoke Aphrodite daughter of
        Zeus:
'Ankhises, greatest in glory of humans doomed to die,
Fill yourself now with courage, and don't be so frightened at
        heart.
You've no reason to fear that you'll suffer some evil inflicted
        by me
Or the other blessed immortals, since you are dear to the
        gods.
You will have a son of your own, who amongst the Trojans
        will rule,
And children descended from him will never lack children
        themselves.
His name will be *Aineias*, since a *dreadful* pain
Has seized me, because I fell into the bed of a mortal man.   199
    But those who in form and appearance most resemble the
        gods
Amongst humans doomed to die have always sprung from
        your race.
Sagacious Zeus, indeed, because of his beauty snatched
Blond Ganymedes away, amongst the immortals to live
And within the abode of Zeus to pour out drink for the gods.
It's a wonder to see him there, by all the immortals esteemed,
As he draws the ruddy nektar from his golden bowl.
But unforgettable sorrow was gripping Tros at heart,
And he had no notion at all of where his beloved son
Was brought when the stormwind sent from heaven snatched
        him away;   208
So then for him he was making constant, unending lament.
Zeus took pity and gave him horses with nimble hooves,
Of the sort that convey the immortals, as payment for his son.
These he gave him to keep as a gift; and at Zeus' command
The Conductor, the Slayer of Argos, told him all he desired,
How his son was now deathless and ageless, exactly as are the
        gods.
When he heard the message of Zeus, no longer did Tros
        lament,

But within his heart felt gladness; and in his gladness he drove
A chariot pulled by the horses with hooves moving swift as the
    storm.
    And so too by golden-throned Dawn was Tithonos
    snatched away,   218
A man who was sprung from your race, who resembled the
    deathless gods.
And Dawn went to seek as a favour from Kronos' black-
    clouded son
That Tithonos be free of death and live throughout all time;
Zeus gave her his nod in promise, and brought her wish to
    pass.
But the thought never entered the head of queenly Dawn (the
    fool!)
To ask that Zeus grant him youth and strip off him destructive
    age.
So long then as he remained possessed of gorgeous youth,
Delighting in Dawn whose throne is golden, the early-born,
He dwelt by Ocean's streams at the outermost limits of Earth.
But when the first grey hairs appeared on his handsome
    head   229
And grew in his noble beard, away then from his bed
Queenly Dawn was staying, but kept him within her halls
And nursed him with food and ambrosia, giving him beautiful
    clothes.
But when he was fully bowed under the weight of hateful age,
And was not able to move or raise a single limb,
Then the best course to adopt seemed to Dawn in her heart to
    be this:
She set him down in a chamber, and closed the gleaming
    doors.
From him flows ceaseless speech, but he has no vigour left
Of the sort that in former times was found in his pliant limbs.
    I would not have it that you amongst the immortals
    be   240
In this way free of death and live throughout all time.
If in form and build you could live as you are, and be called
    my spouse,

Then the shrewd mind within me would not be enfolded by
      grief.
But merciless, levelling age will soon be enfolding you now,
That never departs from humans when once beside them it
      stands,
Old age that wastes and wearies, shuddered at even by gods.
But a great disgrace will be mine amongst the immortal gods
For ever, throughout all time, that I'll suffer because of you.
Before today they feared the murmurs and cunning plans
That I used to join together at some stage every god   250
In love with mortal women: my thought subdued them all.
But now I'll have no longer this boast on my lips to tell
Amongst the immortals, since into an act of pure folly, perverse,
That I can't bear to name, I've been tricked, been led astray
      from my wits,
And under my girdle conceived a child in a mortal's bed.
      As soon as he sees the Sun's light, the nymphs with
        ample breasts
Who inhabit this tall, divine mountain will bring the child up
      in their care.
They follow neither mortals nor immortal gods;
Long is the span of their lives, and deathless the food that they
      eat;
And amongst the immortal gods in beautiful dance they
      swirl.   261
They join with Seilenoi in love in the nooks of enticing caves,
And the keen-eyed Slayer of Argos is also joined with them
      there.
Fir-trees and high-topped oaks on the earth that nurtures men
Sprout at the birth of these nymphs; the trees with beautiful
      growth
Stand tall on the lofty mountains—immortals' precincts they're
      called,
And no mortals hew them with iron. But when the doom of
      death
Beside the nymphs is standing, first the beautiful trees
Dry up in the earth, the bark shrivels round them, their
      boughs fall down,

And it's then that the souls of the nymphs depart the light of
     the Sun.
These nymphs, keeping with them my child, will bring him
     up in their care.   273
    As soon as upon him comes the time of gorgeous youth,
Here will the goddesses bring and show to you the child.
But I, to inform you further of all the plans in my mind,
After four years have passed shall return, bringing with me our
     son.
As soon as you set your eyes upon this offshoot of ours,
You'll be filled with joy at the sight, for he'll be very like the
     gods;
And you at once will bring him to Ilios swept by the wind.
If any of mortal men inquire who the mother may be
That under her girdle conceived a beloved son for you,
To him let you, remembering, answer as I command: 283
    "They say he's the offspring born of a nymph with
      budding face,
One of those who have as their home this mountain that forest
     clothes."
    But if with a senseless heart you speak and make it your
     boast
That you were joined with Kythera's fair-crowned goddess in
     love,
Zeus in his anger will blast you with thunder's smouldering
     bolt.
To you now all has been spoken; let you, taking thought in
     your mind,
Desist, don't utter my name, but dread the wrath of the gods.'
    When she had in this way spoken, she shot to the wind-
     swept sky.
    Farewell to you, goddess who over firm-founded Cyprus
     reign.
From you I began; I will now move on to another hymn.   293

Hymn 6: To Aphrodite

I will sing of that beautiful goddess who wears a crown of
  gold,
Revered Aphrodite, who owns on all Cyprus surrounded by
  sea
Each circling head-dress of towers. There strong Zephyr's
  moist breath
Through crashing waves conveyed her, amid the soft foam, to
  shore.
The Seasons whose fillets are golden gave her a welcome of
  joy,
And wrapped her in deathless clothes. Upon her immortal
  head
They placed a beautiful crown of exquisite craft in gold;
With flowers of mountain's copper and costly gold they
  pierced
The lobes of her ears; and about her soft neck and gleaming
  breasts
They adorned her with chains of gold, of the sort in which
  they themselves,   11
The Seasons whose fillets are golden, would both go adorned
  to the gods'
Lovely dance and their father's abode. But then, her
  adornment complete,
They led her amongst the immortals, and they were amazed at
  the sight.
They gave her their right hands in greeting, and each god
  prayed that she be
His own wedded wife to bring home, so amazed were they at
  the form
Of Kythera's goddess who wears a crown of the violet's bloom.
  Farewell to you, black-eyed goddess whose spirit is sweet
    and kind;
In the contest permit this bard to win, and make ready my
  song.
But I will call to my mind both you and another song.   21

HYMN 7: TO DIONYSOS

Concerning Dionysos, glorious Semele's son,
I'll remember how once he appeared by the shore of the
      murmuring sea
Upon a jutting headland, in looks like a young man whose
      prime
Has just begun; the beautiful hair that round him waved
Was dark, and round his sturdy shoulders he wore a cloak
Of purple. Soon men on a ship benched well for rowers
      arrived,
Pirates moving swiftly over the wine-dark sea,
Tyrsenians, led by an evil doom. At the sight of him there
They gave each other the nod, and soon leaped out. In haste
They seized and set him on board their ship, exultant at
      heart.   10
For they said that he was the son of kings who are cherished
      by Zeus,
And wanted him cruelly bound. But their bonds could not
      hold him, far
From his hands and feet the withies kept falling, while there
      he sat,
And with his dark eyes smiled. The helmsman, perceiving the
      truth,
Called aloud to his comrades without delay, and said:
    'Misguided men, what mighty god is this you seize
And bind? Our ship cannot even bear him, built well though
      she be.
For Zeus is here, or Apollo, God of the Silver Bow,
Or Poseidon: these are no looks of mortal men, but of gods
Who dwell in Olympian homes. Now come, let's set him
      ashore   22
On the land's black soil at once. Against him raise no hand,
In case he stirs in wrath cruel winds of hurricane force.'
    In this way he spoke; the captain rebuked him with
      hateful words:
'Misguided man, keep watch for the breeze, and then raise the
      ship's sail,

With all the ropes in your grasp; this fellow will worry us men.
He is, I expect, for either Egypt or Cyprus bound,
Or else for the Hyperboreans, or further afield. In the end
At some point he'll tell us his kith and kin, and all their
    wealth,
And who his brothers are, since heaven has sent him to us.'
    With these words he started to raise the mast and sail of
    the ship.   32
A wind bellied out the sail, and on every side they stretched
The ropes taut; but soon before them miraculous works
    appeared.
Wine at first began along the swift, black ship
To gurgle, sweet to the taste and fragrant—the scent that rose
    up
Was divine—and all the sailors were seized with awe at the
    sight.
But at once on either side along the topmost edge
Of the sail a vine was stretched out, and grapes were hanging
    down
In clusters; dark-green ivy twined about the mast,
Bursting with bloom; upon it delightful berries stirred,
And all the tholes were wearing garlands. The men, when they
    saw,   42
Then indeed kept bidding the helmsman to steer the ship
Toward shore; but the god within their ship became at the
    prow
A fearsome lion, roaring loud, and amidships made
A bear with shaggy-maned neck, revealing his portents to
    view.
It reared up fiercely, the lion upon the upper deck

.   .   .   .

Shooting a fearsome glare; the men fled back to the stern,
And on every side of the helmsman who had a prudent heart
They stood in terror. The god with a sudden rush forward
    seized
The captain; the men, as they tried to escape from an evil
    doom,
All together plunged, when they saw, in the brilliant sea,   52

And into dolphins turned. But holding the helmsman back
In pity, he made him in all ways blessed, and spoke these words:
    'Take courage, noble father, you who have pleased my
       heart.
I am Dionysos who roars out loud, and was given birth
By Semele, Kadmos' child, who was joined in love with Zeus.'
    Farewell to you, fair-faced Semele's offspring. It cannot
      be
That one forgetful of you arrays a song that is sweet.   59

HYMN 8: TO ARES

Ares surpassing in might, who weigh the chariot down,
Who wear a helmet of gold and possess a spirit of strength,
Shield-bearing saviour of cities, clothed in armour of bronze,
Whose mighty hand unwearied wields a spear that is strong,
Olympos' bulwark, father of Victory skilful in war,
You who bring help to Themis, you who are tyrant to foes,
You who are leader of humans who cherish justice most,
Sceptred king of valour who whirl a fire-bright orb
Amongst the portents of heaven that wander along seven paths,
Where blazing colts keep you for ever beyond the third rim of
    the sky!   8
Pay heed, you ally of mortals, giver of flourishing youth,
And from on high shed down a gentle light on our life
And martial strength to give me power to drive from my head
The bitter taint of cowardice, power to thwart with my mind
The soul's deceitful impulse, and power besides to hold back
The fierce might of spirit that pricks me to enter chill strife—
    but grant,
Blessed One, courage to stay in the painless laws of peace,
Evading the enemies' broil and the violent spirits of death.   17

HYMN 9: TO ARTEMIS

Sing, Muse, of Artemis, sister of him who shoots from afar,
The virgin archeress reared with Apollo. Her horses' thirst
She slakes in Meles' reed-choked stream, and quickly then
    drives

Through Smyrna her car of pure gold to Klaros where vines
    abound.
There Apollo is sitting, god of the silver bow,
Awaiting his archeress sister, the goddess who shoots from
    afar.
    So may you with every goddess take parting joy in my
        song!
But you are my song's first theme, and from you I begin to
    sing;
From you I began; I will now move on to another hymn.   9

Hymn 10: To Aphrodite

Of the Native of Cyprus, Kythera's goddess, I'll sing. She gives
To mortals soothing gifts, and upon her desirable face
Has always a smile, while upon her plays a desirable bloom.
    Farewell to you, goddess who over firm-founded Salamis
        reign
And sea-surrounded Cyprus; grant desirable song.
But I will call to my mind both you and another song.   6

Hymn 11: To Athena

With Pallas Athena, protectress of cities, my song begins,
With that fearsome goddess who cares with Ares for warlike
    works—
The sacking of cities, the scream of battle, the clash of the fray—
And also ensures the army's safe parting and homeward
    return.
    Farewell to you, goddess! Grant us success and prosperous
        life.   5

Hymn 12: To Hera

Of Hera I sing, whose throne is golden, whom Rhea bore,
The immortal Queen, beyond compare in beauty of form,
The glorious sister and spouse of Zeus who thunders loud,
Whom all the blessed gods upon tall Olympos rank
In dread and honour as equal to Zeus whom thunder
    delights.   5

HYMN 13: TO DEMETER

With fair-tressed Demeter, the sacred goddess, my song
    begins,
With herself and also her daughter, Persephoneia most fair.
    Farewell, goddess! Keep this city safe, and begin the
      song.   3

HYMN 14: TO THE MOTHER OF THE GODS

Hymn the Mother from whom all gods and humans come,
I ask you, clear-voiced Muse, you daughter of mighty Zeus.
The noise of rattles and drums delights her, the wailing too
Of flutes, the howling of wolves and the bright-eyed lions'
    roar,
The mountains where echoes resound and the valleys where
    forests grow.
    So may you with every goddess take parting joy in my
      song!   6

HYMN 15: TO HERAKLES THE LIONHEART

Of Herakles, son of Zeus, I will sing, the best by far
Of humans on earth, whom at Thebes where the dancing-
    grounds are fair
Alkmene bore, having joined with Kronos' black-clouded son.
In the past, while wandering over land beyond measure and sea
On missions imposed upon him by King Eurystheus' command,
He did much that was reckless himself, but also had much to
    endure;
Yet now on the beautiful seat of snowy Olympos' peak
Taking delight he dwells, and has fair-ankled Hebe to wife.
    Farewell to you, lord son of Zeus. May you grant us
      prowess and wealth!   9

HYMN 16: TO ASKLEPIOS

With Asklepios, plague-healing son of Apollo, my song begins.
King Phlegyas' child, bright Koronis, gave birth on the Dotion
    plain

To this great joy for humans who charms ill pangs away.
 And so farewell to you, lord; I pray to you in song.   5

HYMN 17: TO THE SONS OF ZEUS

Of Kastor and Polydeukes sing, you clear-voiced Muse,
Of Tyndareos' sons who were born of Olympian Zeus. To
     them
Under the peaks of Taÿgetos queenly Leda gave birth,
After being in secret tamed under Kronos' black-clouded son.
 Farewell to you, sons of Tyndareos, mounted upon swift
     steeds.   5

HYMN 18: TO HERMES

Of Hermes, Kyllenian god and Slayer of Argos, I sing,
Who over Kyllene reigns and Arkadia rich in flocks,
The immortals' speedy messenger. Maia gave him birth,
Atlas' daughter, having joined in love with Zeus,
Being worthy of reverence. Shunning the throng of blessed
     gods,
She dwelt in a deep-shaded cave, where Kronos' son used to
     join
With the nymph whose tresses are fair at the milking-time of
     night,
While Hera whose arms are pale in the sweetness of sleep was
     clasped,
And neither immortal gods nor mortal humans knew.
 And so farewell I bid you, Zeus and Maia's son.   10
From you I began; I will now move on to another hymn.
Farewell to you, Grace-Giver Hermes, Conductor, Giver of
     Good.   12

HYMN 19: TO PAN

Concerning Hermes' beloved offspring speak to me, Muse,
That goat-hooved, two-horned lover of clamour who roams
     through meads
Of woodland together with nymphs whose nature it is to dance.
Down peaks of rugged rock they tread and call on Pan,

The squalid god of pasture with splendid hair, who owns
Each snowy ridge, the mountains' summits and rocky ways.
> He roams through tangled thickets, passing now here,
> now there.
Sometimes soft streams entice him, but sometimes he strays on
> sheer rocks,
Ascending the height of a summit that stands on guard over
> flocks.
Often he races through mountains that rear up white and
> tall;
Often he drives in the valleys wild beasts in deadly pursuit,
While keeping sharp watch about him; but then at evening
> alone
He returns from the hunt, and in sport sounds out a sweet
> tune on his pipes—
Not even that bird could surpass him in music which sits
> among leaves
In springtime, when flowers aplenty are blooming, and pours
> out her dirge
In gushes of honey-voiced song. And with him then nimbly
> roam
The clear-singing nymphs of the mountain; by dark spring
> waters they sing
In strains whose moaning echo embraces the mountain's peak.
On this side and that of the choirs, and then right into their
> midst,
The god moves nimbly in charge; a tawny lynx-hide he
> wears,
And exults in his mind at their songs that ring clear through
> the soft meadow-field,
Where the crocus and fragrant hyacinth bloom beyond count
> in the grass.
> They hymn the blessed gods and their high Olympian
> home,
And one such hymn that they sing is of Hermes peerless in
> speed.
They tell how for all the immortals he as swift messenger
> serves,

12

24

And once to Arkadia came, where many fountains flow,
The mother of flocks, and where his Kyllenian precinct stands.
There, though a god, he pastured a mortal's rough-fleeced
　　　flocks,
For coming upon him the tender desire grew strong, to be
　　　joined
In love with the daughter of Dryops, a bride whose tresses
　　　were fair.　　　　　　　　　　　　　　　　　　34
He brought their fruitful marriage to pass, and at once she
　　　bore
In the halls for Hermes—portentous to see—his beloved son,
A goat-hooved, two-horned maker of clamour whose laughter
　　　is sweet.
But, springing up, she fled, and left her child to the nurse;
For she quailed at the sight of his face that was fierce and
　　　covered with beard.
But speedy Hermes received him, clasped him at once in his
　　　arms,
And rejoiced in his mind beyond measure. With hides of the
　　　mountain hare
He wrapped the child close, and approached in haste the
　　　immortals' abodes.
He sat beside Zeus and the other immortals, and showed
　　　them his son;
They all were pleased at heart, Dionysos Bakkheios the most,46
And *Pan* was the name that they gave him for pleasing the
　　　hearts of them *all*.
　　And so farewell to you, lord; I give you appeasement in
　　　song.
But I will call to my mind both you and another song.　　　49

HYMN 20: TO HEPHAISTOS

Sing, you clear-voiced Muse, of Hephaistos renowned for craft,
Who with bright-eyed Athena taught splendid works to
　　　humans on earth—
They had before then been dwelling in caves on the
　　　mountains like beasts,

But now, knowing works through Hephaistos renowned for his
    skill, with ease
Till the year brings its end they live in comfort within their
    own homes.
    Come now, be kindly, Hephaistos; grant us prowess and
    wealth.   8

HYMN 21: TO APOLLO

Of you, Phoibos, even the swan sings clear to the wing-beat's
    tune
As he lights on the bank by Peneios' eddying stream; and of you
The sweet bard with clear-sounding lyre sings ever both first
    and last.
    And so farewell to you, lord; I give you appeasement in
    song.   5

HYMN 22: TO POSEIDON

Concerning Poseidon, that mighty god, I begin to sing,
Who stirs the earth and murmuring sea, the lord of the deep,
Who over Helikon rules and spacious Aigai too.
In twain the gods divided, Shaker of Earth, your share
Of honour—to be the tamer of horses and saviour of ships.
    Farewell, Poseidon, Holder of Earth, whose hair is dark;
Blessed One, kindly at heart, bring help to those who sail.   7

HYMN 23: TO ZEUS

Of Zeus I will make my song, of the best and greatest of gods,
The far-seeing sovereign from whom fulfilment comes. It is he
Who to Themis murmurs wise words while inclining towards
    him she sits.
    Be gracious, Kronos' greatest, most glorious, far-seeing
    son.   4

HYMN 24: TO HESTIA

Hestia, you who at holy Pytho bestow your care
On the sacred abode of the lord, Apollo who shoots from afar,
The locks of your hair are always dripping with liquid oil.

Enter this house, your heart at one with Zeus the wise,
Enter, and grant to my song your favouring grace besides. 　5

Hymn 25: To the Muses, Apollo, and Zeus

From the Muses, Apollo, and Zeus I will make my beginning
　　　of song.
For it is from the Muses and lord Apollo who shoots from afar
That men upon the earth are singers and skilled with the lyre,
And from Zeus that men are kings. But blessed is that man
Who is loved by the Muses: sweet is the voice that flows from
　　　his lips.
　　Farewell to you, children of Zeus, and honour this song
　　　of mine.
But I will call to my mind both you and another song. 　7

Hymn 26: To Dionysos

With the god who has ivy hair, Dionysos who roars out loud,
The splendid son of Zeus whom glorious Semele bore,
I begin to sing. He was reared by nymphs whose tresses are
　　　fair:
From the lord his father they took to their bosom and fostered
　　　with care
This child in the hollows of Nysa. He grew through his
　　　father's will—
Being reckoned amongst the immortals—within a fragrant
　　　cave.
When the goddesses finished his rearing, this god much
　　　honoured in hymns
Through the wooded glens went wandering, covered with ivy
　　　and bay.
Behind him followed the nymphs, in front he was leading the
　　　way,
And, stretched out far beyond telling, the forest rang with his
　　　roar. 　10
　　And so to you farewell, Dionysos rich in grapes.
Permit us to come once more in joy as the seasons return,
And then from season to season for many succeeding years. 　13

HYMN 27: TO ARTEMIS

Of Artemis, goddess with distaff of gold, whose cry resounds,
I sing, the virgin revered, the archeress shooter of deer,
The sister by birth of Apollo, god of the golden sword.
In the chase over shadowy mountains and wind-swept peaks
        she delights,
And takes aim with a bow of pure gold, dispatching arrows of
        woe.
The heads of high mountains tremble, the thick-shaded forest
        screams out
A dire echo of bestial clamour, and shudderings shake both
        the earth
And the sea that is teeming with fish; but she with a heart
        that is strong
Now this way turns, now that, destroying the race of beasts.
Yet when the archeress tracker of beasts has had pleasure
        enough   11
From the hunt and has gladdened her mind, she unstrings her
        flexible bow
And goes to her brother's great home, to Phoibos Apollo's
        abode
In Delphi's rich land, to prepare for the Muses' and Graces'
        fair dance.
She hangs up there with its arrows her bow that springs back
        from the pull,
And wearing graceful adornments takes the lead in the dance.
The goddesses, raising their heavenly voices, sing a hymn
Of fair-ankled Leto, and tell how she gave her children birth,
Who are in both counsel and deeds the best of immortals by
        far.
     Farewell to you, children of Zeus and Leto with lovely hair;
But I will call to my mind both you and another song.   22

HYMN 28: TO ATHENA

With Pallas Athena, that glorious goddess, my song begins,
Who is bright-eyed, rich in craft, who has an implacable heart,

The virgin revered, protectress of cities, possessor of strength,
Tritogenes. It was Craft-filled Zeus himself who gave birth
From his sacred head to her already in armour of war,
Golden, all-gleaming; every immortal was gripped with awe
At the sight. But quickly she leaped from his deathless head to
    stand
Before Zeus who bears the *aigis*, and brandished her keen-
    tipped spear.
At the might of the bright-eyed goddess great Olympos reeled
In a fearsome tremor, the earth all round with a dreadful
    scream   11
Rang out, and the deep was stirred in a mass of seething
    waves.
But the salt sea suddenly checked, and Hyperion's splendid
    son
For a long-drawn moment kept still the swift hoofs of his
    chariot's team,
Until from her deathless shoulders Pallas Athena took off
That armour fit for a god, and Craft-filled Zeus rejoiced.
      And so farewell to you, child of *aigis*-bearing Zeus;
But I will call to my mind both you and another song.   18

Hymn 29: To Hestia

Hestia, you who obtained as your lot in the lofty abodes
Of all the immortal gods and of humans who walk on the
    earth
A seat that for ever endures as the honour due to your age,
Possessing a beautiful portion and honour—for not without you
Are banquets held by mortals, where he who begins pours out
No wine as sweet as honey for Hestia first and last.
And you, the Slayer of Argos, Zeus and Maia's son,
The blessed ones' messenger, Giver of Good with rod of gold,
Being gracious, bring me your help with her, revered and dear
Hestia. For you both inhabit the beautiful homes   9
Of humans on earth, being lovingly disposed in mind
To each other; beautiful props, you attend on thought and
    youth.

Farewell to you, Kronos' daughter and Hermes with rod
of gold;
But I will call to my mind both you and another song.   14

HYMN 30: TO EARTH THE MOTHER OF ALL

I will sing of Earth, the Mother of All, whose foundations are
strong,
The eldest of gods, who feeds all creatures that live on the
land—
All those that roam the bright land, all those that swim in the
sea,
All those that take to the wing, your riches feed all these.
From you comes abundance of children and harvests, Queen;
by you
Life's nurture is granted to mortals, and from them is taken
away.
The man whom you honour kindly at heart is blessed: all joys
Are his in bountiful measure. For him the corn weighs down
The ploughland that bears life's nurture, his herds in the
pastures increase,
And his house is filled with treasures. Such men in person
preside   12
In lawful rule over towns where beautiful women dwell,
And much fortune and wealth attends them; their sons exult
in the mirth
Of freshly sprouting youth, and their daughters, cheerful at
heart,
Frolic and skip in garlanded troops through the meadow's soft
blooms—
Such honours, sacred goddess, bountiful power, you give.
Farewell to you, Mother of Gods, the spouse of starry Sky;
In goodwill return for my song life's nurture that pleases the
heart.
But I will call to my mind both you and another song.   19

HYMN 31: TO THE SUN

Begin now, Muse, Kalliope, daughter of Zeus, a hymn
To the beaming Sun, whom cow-eyed Euryphaëssa bore

To the child of Earth and starry Sky. For Hyperion took
That glorious goddess, Euryphaëssa, to be his wife,
His very own sister, who gave his beautiful offspring birth—
The Dawn whose arms are rose-pink, the Moon whose tresses
      are fair,
And the Sun who knows no fatigue, who is all that immortals
      should be.
He shines from his horse-drawn car for mortals and deathless
      gods,
Shooting a fearsome glare from beneath his helmet of gold,
While from him rays of brightness with dazzling radiance
      glow.   11
From his temples brilliant cheek-pieces frame his handsome
      face
As it beams afar, and there blazes fair on his flesh a robe
Of delicate weave in the breath of the winds. The stallions below

   .   .   .   .

It is then that he brings to a halt his gold-yoked car and his
      steeds,
And in godly splendour through heaven sends toward Ocean
      his team.
    Farewell, lord! Provide in goodwill life's nurture that
    pleases the heart.
From you I began; I will now bring fame to the race of men,
To the race of the half-gods, whose deeds the gods have to
      mortals revealed.   19

Hymn 32: To Selene

Of the long-winged Moon give utterance, sweet-spoken Muses,
      to sing,
Young maiden daughters of Kronos' son Zeus, who are skilled
      in song.
The light that in heaven is plain to view is whirled to earth
From her deathless head, and vast is the splendour, rising slow,
Of that light as it shines. Devoid itself of brightness, the air
Takes fire from her crown of gold, and her beams are clear as
      day,

Whenever, emerging from Ocean, her beautiful flesh washed
    clean
And clothed in far-seen robes, resplendent Selene has yoked
Her long-necked, dazzling colts and in haste drives forward at
    dusk
Those horses with beautiful manes at the midway point of the
    month,   11
When her orbit's huge swathe is full, and her rays then from
    heaven most bright,
As still she continues her growth, for mortals a token and sign.
She once with the son of Kronos was joined on the bed of
    love,
Grew pregnant and bore Pandeia, her daughter whose beauty
    of form
Stands out beyond compare amongst the immortal gods.
    Farewell to you, queenly goddess, Selene the pale-armed
    and bright,
Whose heart is full of goodwill, whose tresses are fair. From
    you
I begin; I will now sing the glories of men, of the half-gods
    whose feats
Gain fame from the lovely lips of the Muses' attendants, the
    bards.   20

HYMN 33: TO THE SONS OF ZEUS

Concerning the Sons of Zeus, you black-eyed Muses, speak,
The sons of Tyndareos, fair-ankled Leda's splendid boys—
Kastor tamer of steeds, Polydeukes who has no flaw.
Beneath tall Taÿgetos' peak she gave birth, having joined in love
With Kronos' black-clouded son, to these saviours of earthly
    men
And their speedily faring ships. When wintry tempests rage
Across the implacable deep, in prayer the sailors call
On the Sons of mighty Zeus with white lambs at the edge of
    the stern.
The strong gale and surge of the sea have sent the ship under!
    But now

They come, propelled through the sky on rustling wings. At
    once   14
They still the fierce blasts, and smooth the waves on the
    frothing deep.
Fair signs are these for sailors, and mark their freedom from
    toil;
At the sight the sailors rejoice, and with dismal toil have done.
    Farewell to you, sons of Tyndareos, mounted upon swift
      steeds;
But I will call to my mind both you and another song.   19

To Hosts

Respect the man in need of hospitable gifts and a home,
You folk who dwell within the steep city of Hera, that nymph
Lovely of face, at high-leafed Saidene's lowest foot,
You who have heavenly water to drink, from the yellow stream
Of finely flowing Hermos whom deathless Zeus begot.   5

EXPLANATORY NOTES

Hy. = *Hymn*. A name in capital letters refers to an entry in the Glossary.

Hymn 1: *To Dionysos*

Verses 10–21 of this hymn, together with the whole of *Hy.* 2, are preserved in a single manuscript, which lacks its beginning. It seems likely from its position in this manuscript that *Hy.* 1 was originally comparable in length to *Hymns* 2–5. Verses 1–9 are quoted as being from the *Hymns* of Homer by the first-century BC historian Diodorus Siculus (1. 15. 7; 3. 66. 3; 4. 2. 4), and are assumed to belong to the same hymn as verses 10–21.

A papyrus fragment of a hexameter poem involving Dionysos has also been linked with *Hy.* 1; if this connection is correct, the papyrus fragment reveals the hymn's lost narrative, which can be summarized as follows (Merkelbach 1973: 212–13):

After giving birth to her crippled son Hephaistos, Hera throws him to earth from Olympos in disgust. Hephaistos, god of craftsmen and fire, gets his revenge by making a splendid throne and offering it to his mother as a gift. Once she sits in it, she cannot get up, being gripped by hidden, unbreakable bonds. Her other son, the war-god Ares, tries to force Hephaistos to release their mother, but cannot stand against his brother's flames. Then Dionysos intervenes, promising to appease Hephaistos, on condition that he himself is counted as one of the Olympian gods. Hera had previously refused him this honour, being jealous of his mother Semele; she now has no choice but to recognize Dionysos. The god of wine then goes to Hephaistos, makes him drunk, and brings him back to Olympos; before releasing Hera, Hephaistos demands Aphrodite as his wife.

This story, showing how Dionysos attained his present position, would suit a Homeric hymn; yet, as there is nothing in the surviving text of the hymn that explicitly relates to the tale, the connection of the papyrus fragment with *Hy.* 1 is uncertain.

1–9 *For some say it was on Drakanon . . . near to Egypt's streams*: the poet lists five alleged birthplaces of Dionysos before dismissing them all and settling on a sixth, Mount Nysa. This is an example of the priamel, a figure in which a statement can be

emphasized by being put last in a paratactic series: compare
Hy. 3. 143–8. See West (1978: 269) and the entry under
priamel in *The Oxford Classical Dictionary* (Hornblower and
Spawforth 1996: 1244). Janko (1981: 12–13) points out the
use of the priamel in the *Hymns* as a transitional device often
leading on to a mythic narrative, as seems likely to have been
the case in *Hymn* 1.

6 *You were borne by the Father of men and gods himself*: Hera
tricked Semele into forcing Zeus to appear to her in his true
form; Semele perished when Zeus showed himself as a
thunderbolt; Zeus rescued their unborn child, sewed him
into his thigh, and later gave birth to Dionysos, one of whose
titles is interpreted as 'insewn' (2, 17, 20). Cf. Athena's birth
from Zeus' head (*Hy.* 28. 4–16).

7 *in secret from Hera*: compare the secrecy and remote location
of Hermes' conception and birth at *Hy.* 4. 1–19.

10–11 *And for her they will dedicate many gifts within their shrines.* | *But
as he cut you in three*: the loss of the preceding part of the
poem prevents certainty of interpretation. Zeus is speaking.
'Her' may mean Semele, who becomes a goddess after death
(see 21); 'he' is unknown; 'you' is Dionysos, but is supplied
in the translation to complete the sense, being absent from
the Greek text. The reference seems to be to a story in which
Dionysos is cut into three pieces and subsequently resur-
rected, explaining the origin of triennial festivals in his
honour. Not all editors agree, however, that the Greek text
contains a verb of 'cutting'.

12 *hecatombs*: the word 'hecatomb', *hekatombe* in Greek, is
derived from *hekaton*, a hundred, and *bous*, oxen: it originally
denoted a sacrificial offering of 100 oxen, though it can be
applied to the sacrifice of much smaller numbers.

   every third year: the Greeks counted inclusively; we would say
'every *second* year'.

13–15 *The son of Kronos spoke . . . and he made great Olympos shake*: for
the significance of Zeus' nod see note on *Hy.* 4. 519.

16 *So said sagacious Zeus, and gave the command with his head*: this
verse is redundant, being an alternative for 13–15.

17 *who drive women to madness*: frenzied women are a feature of
Dionysiac myth and worship (see note on 21, and *Hy.* 2. 386).

17–19 *We bards ¦ Sing of you both when . . . remembers sacred song*: see
      note on *Hy.* 2. 495.

   21 *And to her whom they call Thyone, your mother Semele, too*: the
      sense appears to be that mortals ('they') worship Dionysos'
      mother under the title 'Thyone' ('the Frenzied One'),
      Semele being her original and true name. It is not uncom-
      mon in Homeric poetry for the same person or thing to have
      different divine and mortal names.

Hymn 2: *To Demeter*

This hymn has usually been thought to describe the origin of the
Eleusinian Mysteries, which were celebrated annually at Eleusis for
over a millennium, and were based on the story of the abduction of
Persephone (also called simply *Kore*, 'Daughter') by Hades, king of the
dead, and her eventual return to her mother Demeter in the upper world
for two-thirds of the year. The myth explains the coming of spring after
winter, and passes from grief and famine to rejoicing and new growth.
This partial triumph of life over death is reflected in the Mysteries, which
offered initiates an improved lot both in this world and in the afterlife
(see 480–2, 486–9). The hymn does not give a complete blueprint of the
Mysteries and the various stages along the path to full initiation in them,
but seems to provide the mythical precedent for several elements of them
(see notes on 47–50, 192–211, 370–4, 476–9). It is remarkable that
there is no mention of Athens in the poem, given its proximity to Eleusis
and the fact that one of the main features of the Mysteries from at least
the start of the fifth century BC was a procession to Eleusis from Athens: a
possible explanation is that the poem was composed before the
Mysteries came under direct Athenian control—but see Clinton
(1993: 110–12). Janko (1982: 200) dates the hymn to *c*.645–630 BC;
note also Richardson (1974: 5–11). For a succinct presentation of what
is known about the Mysteries see Burkert (1985: 285–90). See also Clay
(1989: 202–66) and Parker (1991).

   The connection between the hymn and the Eleusinian Mysteries has
been called into question: Clinton (1993: 113–15), although accepting
that the poem does refer to the Mysteries at 473–82, argues that at
other points it is more closely linked to the Thesmophoria festival—on
which see Burkert (1985: 242–6).

    5 *Ocean's full-bosomed daughters*: these are listed in full when
      Persephone recounts to her mother the tale of her abduction
      (417–24).

6 *plucking flowers*: maidens in myth are often carried off whilst
engaged in this occupation. Here the contrast between
Persephone's innocent, girlish activity and the sudden
eruption of the god of the dead is particularly effective. Cf.
Milton, *Paradise Lost* IV. 268–72:

> Not that fair field
> Of Enna, where Proserpine gathering flowers
> Herself a fairer flower by gloomy Dis
> Was gathered, which cost Ceres all that pain
> To seek her through the world . . .

(Proserpine = Persephone; Dis = Hades; Ceres = Demeter.)
Milton follows later sources in locating the abduction at
(H)enna in Sicily.

6–8 *the rose,* | *The crocus and beautiful violet, iris and hyacinth
blooms,* | *And narcissus*: the flowers chosen may not be without
significance (Richardson 1974: 140–4). The rose, violet, and
iris were used to decorate graves; the crocus was associated
with Demeter; the hyacinth was a product of death, having
been created from the blood of the slain Hyakinthos; and
narcissus (an actual flower, though the specimen that tempts
Persephone is preternatural) was connected with the underworld. While some—crocus, violet, narcissus—are known to
occur in Greece in varieties that bloom in autumn, the
appropriate time for Persephone's abduction, the poet
probably did not select them with a strict eye to chronology.

19 *his golden car*: here and elsewhere in the translation 'car'
denotes a chariot.

23 *the olives with sparkling fruit*: it seems peculiar that olives
should be mentioned here together with gods and humans
as not having heard Persephone's cry; it has been suggested
that what is meant is a type of Nymph associated with olives.
However, talking trees are not unknown in later poetry and
folk-tale, and olives might be expected to show concern for
the daughter of the goddess of agriculture and to pass on to
Demeter any information that they might have (note the
olive growing by the Maiden's Well at 100).

37 *So long did hope soothe her mighty mind despite her grief*: a lacuna
must be marked after this verse because a description is

lacking of Persephone's descent into the earth and her last, despairing cry, which Demeter hears at 39.

43   *both firm and fluid*: i.e. land and sea.

47–50 *For nine days then queenly Deo . . . nor with bath-water splashed her flesh*: the Mysteries at Eleusis seem to have involved a re-enactment, with torches, of Demeter's search for her daughter; fasting and not washing, common symptoms of extreme grief in Homeric poetry, may also have been part of the Mysteries for initiates imitating the goddess. See Richardson (1974: 162, 165–7), but note also Clay (1989: 217).

63   *his horses*: see note on *Hy.* 31. 14.

86   *when the three-way division was made*: the allusion is to the division of the universe between Zeus, Poseidon, and Hades after the Titans had been overthrown: when the lots were drawn, Zeus got the sky, Poseidon the sea, and Hades the underworld—earth and Olympos remained their common property (*Iliad* 15. 187–93).

91–7 *She then was filled with anger . . . of fragrant Eleusis then*: Demeter's angry withdrawal from divine society with its disastrous consequences for agriculture, and eventually for the gods themselves, can be compared to Hera's withdrawal which produces Typhaon, a monster who threatens the rule of Zeus (*Hy.* 3. 305–55). The appearance of a god in disguise amongst humans is also a common motif in Greek myth.

103   *doom-dealing*: occurring also at 215 and 473, this expression (in which 'doom' is used in the sense of 'decree' or 'statute') is only a rough approximation to the Greek word *themisto-polos*, which means something like 'attending to the oral precedents (*themistes*)'. In the absence of a written law-code, kings and other judges preserve in their memory the *themistes*, from which they pick the most suitable to guide them in judging individual cases (Richardson 1974: 182–3; Janko 1992: 366).

119–44 *Dear children, whoever you are . . . and could teach the women their tasks*: compare Demeter's false tale with that of Aphrodite at *Hy.* 5. 108–42 (she too claims to have been abducted, though by Hermes rather than pirates), and note also Apollo's deception of the Cretans at *Hy.* 3. 448–62.

123 *from Crete*: while some have conjectured that Demeter's
claim to be a Cretan reflects a Cretan origin of the
Eleusinian Mysteries, the poet may merely be following
the precedent of the *Odyssey*, where Odysseus several times
falsely claims to be from Crete (13. 256–86, 14. 199–359,
19. 165–202). By the sixth century BC the Cretans had
acquired a reputation for dishonesty, but this may derive
from Odysseus' false tales rather than explain the Cretan
element in them. The island perhaps had a certain mystique
due to dim recollections of the period of Cretan dominance
in the Aegean area (the 'Minoan' civilization was at its
height *c*.2000–1470 BC); for the purposes of a false tale it
had the advantage of being famous but at the same time far
enough away to make discovery of the falsehood unlikely
(Càssola 1975: 473).

125 *Pirate men*: piracy was common in the Mediterranean from
earliest times. In Homeric poetry it is not viewed as
altogether dishonourable, no more so than cattle-rustling:
Odysseus himself engages in piratical activity at *Odyssey* 9.
39–61. See *Hy*. 3. 453–5 and *Hy*. 7, in which Dionysos
allows himself to be captured by pirates.

137 *but, maidens, take pity on me*: a lacuna is marked after these
words, as the sense does not flow smoothly. A verse
conveying some such request as 'Tell me what I ask'
seems to be required.

145 *the maiden as yet untamed*: see note on *Hy*. 17. 4.

147–8 *Mother, the gifts that the gods . . . for they are more mighty by far*:
this submissive sentiment is repeated below at 216–17. To
avoid incurring divine wrath, humans must always remember their own inferior position. The gulf between the happy
existence of the undying gods and the suffering of witless
mortals is made clear at *Hy*. 3. 189–93.

159 *for you have the look of a god*: cf. *Hy*. 3. 464–5 and *Hy*. 5. 92–
106. Although Demeter's disguise is much more convincing
than that of either Apollo or Aphrodite, the motif whereby
the mortal interlocutor nearly sees through the god's deception is still evident.

188–90 *But onto the threshold stepped . . . awe, and pallid fear*: as the
threshold separates the outside world from the space inside
the house, the act of crossing it is obviously significant; this

is why it is the location of Demeter's transient epiphany (Richardson 1974: 209). The onlookers get a disturbing glimpse of the goddess' true nature, but one that is too brief for them to understand. (Compare Aphrodite's epiphany at *Hy.* 5. 173–5, where the head of that goddess also reaches the roof-beam, and beauty shines from her.)

192–211 *But Demeter, Bringer of Seasons . . . most queenly Deo received*: this passage seems to provide the mythical origin of some important ritual elements of the Eleusinian Mysteries (Richardson 1974: 211–26):

(i) Preliminary purification of the candidate for initiation. This involved sitting silently, head veiled, on a stool that was covered with a fleece. (A ram's head was placed under the candidate's feet, but this is not mentioned in the hymn.)

(ii) A fast, broken by drinking not wine, but a mixture of barley, water, and mint called *kykeon* in the Greek text (often Latinized as *cyceon*).

(iii) Scurrility and comic licence, represented by the joking of Iambe. This distraction from sorrow is the prerequisite for the breaking of the fast. Iambe is the eponym of *iambic* poetry, the original function of which seems to have been to purvey comic abuse in ritual contexts. In another version of the story Iambe is replaced by a figure called Baubo, who makes Demeter laugh by indecently exposing herself to her.

After 211 a lacuna is marked, as the text does not reveal what Demeter does with the *kykeon* prepared at her request. Presumably she drinks it, though it is unusual in Homeric poetry for a god to partake of anything other than ambrosia and nektar (see note on *Hy.* 4. 115–33).

215 *doom-dealing*: see note on 103.

216–17 *But come, the gifts that the gods . . . for upon our neck lies the yoke*: see note on 147–8.

227–30 *Rear him I shall, and it's not . . . to ward off a baneful spell*: Demeter promises magical protection for the infant Demo- phoon from illnesses inflicted through magic; her words show the repetition and careful ordering of an incantation (Richardson 1974: 229). The terms 'cutter of roots', 'strong counter-cut', and 'cutter of wood' refer to the cutting of plants for magical purposes. Cf. Virgil's *Aeneid* 4. 513–14, where Dido, having lost Aeneas, has recourse to magic: 'and herbs that were reaped by moonlight with sickles of bronze are sought, juicy with milk of black poison'. Cf. also *Hy.* 4. 37–8, where a living tortoise is said to be a lucky charm against evil spells.

235 *and he grew like a god*: compare Demophoon's swift growth with the miraculous infancies of Apollo (*Hy.* 3. 120–39) and Hermes (*Hy.* 4. 17–19).

236 *Neither tasting then food nor milk*: a lacuna is marked after these words, as some reference to day seems necessary to balance 'But by night . . .' at the start of 239.

237–41 *With ambrosia she would anoint him . . . and in looks resembled the gods*: Demeter performs three actions in her attempt to make Demophoon immortal:

(i) She anoints him with ambrosia. Although usually presented as the solid food of the gods, ambrosia ('deathless stuff') is at times used as an unguent, and has been described as the divine counterpart to olive oil, just as nektar answers to wine.
(ii) She breathes upon him while clasping him to her bosom. In the Homeric epics the breath of a god gives strength to the hero whom it enters.
(iii) She puts him in the fire at night. This is intended to burn away the child's mortal parts.

In the *Argonautica* of Apollonius Rhodius (4. 869–79) the goddess Thetis tries to immortalize her infant son Akhilleus in a similar way, and with the same lack of success—the process is aborted when an uncomprehending mortal witness (Peleus, Thetis' husband) stupidly cries out. See Richardson (1974: 231–42); note also Clay (1989: 225–6), who argues that Demeter's attempt to immortalize Demophoon is an act of defiance against Zeus comparable to Hera's conception of Typhaon at *Hy.* 3. 305–55.

259 *For let the gods' oath know this, the implacable water of Styx*: see note on *Hy.* 4. 519 concerning the oath by the water of Styx.

265–7 *And in due season for him . . . war and dreadful strife*: the reference is to a festival held at Eleusis called the *Balletys*, at which a mock battle was performed (perhaps consisting of stone-throwing). Some have suggested that the hymn itself was first recited at the Balletys, but others connect it with the Eleusinia, a more important festival also held at Eleusis. See Richardson (1974: 12, 245–7) and the entry under *Eleusinia* in *The Oxford Classical Dictionary* (Hornblower and Spawforth 1996: 520).

268–74 *I am the goddess Demeter . . . you might appease my mind*: Apollo similarly declares his identity and gives instructions for his worship at *Hy.* 3. 480–501; cf. also *Hy.* 7. 56–7.

275–83 *When so she had spoken, the goddess . . . Her darling boy from the floor*: a full epiphany occurs (foreshadowed at 188–90), containing many of the typical signs of a deity's presence: an increase in size and beauty, a youthful appearance, a heavenly perfume, streaming hair, brilliant light, and feelings of fear and awe in the human onlooker. Cf. *Hy.* 3. 440–50 and *Hy.* 5. 172–82.

344–5 *who had to the blessed gods'* | *Unbearable deeds replied by devising her deadly scheme*: the Greek text at this point is corrupt, and the sense uncertain.

370–4 *In this way he spoke, to the joy . . . she would not for ever stay*: Hades, to ensure that Persephone will return to him, sees to it that she eats a pomegranate's seed. It is a widespread notion that you must stay with the dead if you eat their food—by sharing sustenance with them you join their community. A meal is also a common way of ending a marriage-ceremony, and so Persephone's eating of the seed may consummate her union with Hades. The pomegranate, because of its inner redness, can symbolize blood and death; because of its many seeds, it can also represent fertility and marriage. Eating the pomegranate was forbidden to initiates at Eleusis, and in the Thesmophoria festival there was a prohibition against eating pomegranate seeds that fell to the ground. See Allen, Halliday, and Sikes (1936: 168–70) and Richardson (1974: 276).

386 *a raving Maenad*: I have introduced the word 'raving' into the translation in order to convey the force of the name *Maenad*, 'Madwoman', which denotes a frenzied female worshipper of Dionysos.

387–404 *[From the] other [side] Persephone . . . duped you by means of what trick?*: the sense is clear: Persephone jumps down from the chariot and embraces her mother; Demeter asks her if she

ate any food in the underworld; if she did, then she will have
to spend one-third of every year with Hades, returning to the
world above in spring. Here and at 462–79 the single
manuscript that preserves the end of *Hy.* 1 and all of *Hy.* 2
is torn; in the later passage it is possible to fill in the gaps
with more confidence than here (the most mutilated part of
462–79 repeats 444–7 almost exactly).

404 *And the mighty [Receiver of Many] duped you by means of what
     trick?*: the lack of connection in sense between this and the
     previous verse suggests the presence of a lacuna.

413 *And using violence forced me to taste it against my will*: when the
     incident itself is described at 371–4, no violence is men-
     tioned, only secrecy. Commentators suggest that Perse-
     phone 'protests too much'. Perhaps she is unwilling to
     admit to foolishness in having accepted voluntarily the
     pomegranate's seed; or perhaps she accepted the seed
     because she had become reconciled to being Hades' bride,
     but cannot now bring herself to confess this to her mother;
     or perhaps the poet, feeling that an emphasis on violence
     would make implausible the element of secrecy at 371–4
     (Hermes is standing by to take Persephone away), postpones
     the reference to violence until it can be more safely intro-
     duced.

418–24 *Leukippe and Phaino were there . . . and archeress Artemis too*:
     Persephone lists the daughters of Ocean (Oceanids) referred
     to at 5 above, and reveals that Athena and Artemis were also
     present at her abduction. This is an abridged version (with
     some additions) of the list of Oceanids in Hesiod's *Theogony*
     (349–61); such catalogues of names, whether of places or
     mythical figures, were a traditional feature of early Greek
     poetry (see e.g. *Hy.* 3. 30–44, 421–9).

     The presence of Athena and Artemis is intriguing. In
     another version of the story they chase after Hades and try to
     foil his abduction of Persephone, but Zeus checks them with
     his thunderbolt, which opens up the earth and facilitates
     Hades' escape. There are traces, however, of yet another
     version, in which the two goddesses actually collaborate with
     Zeus and Hades. See Richardson (1974: 290–1).

450 *an udder of ploughland*: used also in the *Iliad* (9. 141, 283), this
     metaphor denotes an area of exceptionally fertile soil.

462–79 *[that he would give]* \ *[Such] honours . . . is curbed by the gods' great awe*: see note on 387–404.

473 *doom-dealing*: see note on 103.

476–9 *And disclosed sacred actions to all . . . is curbed by the gods' great awe*: initiates were forbidden, on pain of death, to reveal the inner core of the Mysteries; the code of secrecy was well observed.

476 *And disclosed sacred actions to all*: at this point in the Greek text a verse occurs which expands on 'to all': 'to Triptolemos and Polyxeinos, and besides these to Diokles'. It is usually regarded as spurious due to its infelicitous repetition of 474.

480–2 *Blessed is he who has seen them . . . down in the mouldy gloom*: together with 486–9 these verses promise to initiates in the Eleusinian Mysteries advantages over non-initiates both in life and in the afterlife. The great appeal of the Mysteries throughout antiquity lay in the prospect that they offered to everybody of an improved lot in death, which traditionally was unpleasant even for the greatest of heroes (e.g. Akhilleus at *Odyssey* 11. 488–91). This improvement in afterlife conditions for mortals compensates for the failure to immortalize Demophoon, and is only possible due to the obligation on Persephone to spend part of the year in the underworld (Parker 1991: 11).

491 *Over Paros that waters flow round, and Antron where rocks abound*: both the island of Paros and the region of Thessaly where Antron was situated were important centres of Demeter's worship.

495 *But I will call to my mind both you and another song*: this verse is a common concluding transition-formula in the *Hymns* (*Hy.* 3. 546; *Hy.* 4. 580; *Hy.* 6. 21; *Hy.* 10. 6; *Hy.* 19. 49; *Hy.* 25. 7; *Hy.* 27. 22; *Hy.* 28. 18; *Hy.* 29. 14; *Hy.* 30. 19; *Hy.* 33. 19). While its meaning is not completely clear, the most likely sense is that the poet, while not forgetting about the deity who has just been celebrated, will proceed now to another and unrelated song: at *Hy.* 31. 18–19 and *Hy.* 32. 18–20 it is made explicit that the poet intends to pass on from the divine to a heroic theme. The gods are jealous, and poets must be tactful in order not to incur their wrath; at the moment of transition, therefore, the gods are reassured that they are not being forgotten. Note *Hy.* 1. 17–19: 'We

bards¦Sing of you both when we begin and conclude—it cannot be¦That one forgetful of you remembers sacred song.' Remembering the deity is the prerequisite for remembering poetry (cf. *Hy.* 7. 58—9), and the poet will return to the deity at the end of the recitation (cf. *Hy.* 21. 3—4).

The matter might seem to be complicated by another transition-formula: 'From you I began; I will now move on to another *hymn*' (*Hy.* 5. 293; *Hy.* 9. 9; *Hy.* 18. 11). It is not beyond the bounds of possibility that the bards sang several successive hymns addressed to different deities; however, the term 'hymn' (*hymnos* in Greek) is not applied exclusively to poems dedicated to gods: see e.g. *Hy.* 3. 160—1, 'They remember and sing a *hymn* of the men and women of old . . .'.

Hymn 3: *To Apollo*

The unity of this hymn has long been called into question. It has been argued that two originally separate hymns to Apollo have been joined together by an ancient editor or rhapsode, one (the 'Delian' hymn, 1—181) composed for recitation on Delos and describing Apollo's birth on that island, the other (the 'Pythian' hymn, 182—546) intended to be performed at Delphi and dealing with the establishment of Apollo's oracle there (see notes on 140—64, 177—8, 182, 540—3). The suspicion that arises from the dichotomy in content is reinforced by linguistic and stylistic analysis: see Janko (1982: 99—100, 200, 253), who dated the Delian section to *c.*675—660 BC, and the Pythian to *c.*585 BC. However, the idea that the poem is a unity has gained ground among scholars: see Miller (1986: 111—17), Clay (1989: 17—94), and Janko (1991: 12—13). Certainly, if the hymn is not a unity, it seems as if the later section—usually judged to be the Pythian, though West (1975: 162—5) argues for the opposite view—was composed by someone with knowledge of the earlier: compare 2—13 with 182—206, 19—29 with 207—15, and see notes on 67, 82, 127—32, 216—99.

According to a scholium on Pindar, *Nemean Odes* 2. 1, the author of this hymn was Kynaithos (Cynaethus), one of the Homeridai of Khios: see West (1975), Janko (1982: 102, 113—15), and note on 165—76.

18 *the palm*: see note on 117—19.

30—46 *As many folk as Crete . . . to furnish her son with a home*: such catalogues of names are a traditional feature of early Greek poetry (see e.g. *Hy.* 2. 417—24, *Hy.* 3. 421—9; note also the famous Catalogue of Ships in the *Iliad*'s second book). This catalogue begins as if to outline the extent of Apollo's worship, and only at the end does it become clear that the places listed are those through which Leto passes in her search for a land willing to be the site of Apollo's birth.

67 *someone exceedingly reckless*: the term translated as 'reckless', *atasthalos*, is frequently associated with *hubris* (outrageous, dishonouring, often violent behaviour): both words characterize those who disregard the established order and what is right. At the start of the hymn Apollo's approach inspires fear in the gods, a fear which turns out to be groundless (2– 13). Previously Heaven had been overthrown by his son Kronos; Kronos in turn was toppled by his son Zeus; when Zeus begets a powerful male child there is the possibility that he himself will also be ousted, and Apollo, if he does turn out to be *atasthalos*, might be the one to try it. But Apollo is the opposite of the figure predicted by rumour: Themis, the personification of Righteousness, gives him his first taste of nektar and ambrosia (124–5); in his first utterance he accepts his subordination to Zeus ('And for humans let me proclaim the unerring counsel of Zeus', 132); and when he chooses Delphi as the site of his oracle, he kills there the monstrous Snake that had nursed Typhaon, Hera's prodigious offspring who was conceived in rebellion to Zeus and threatened his rule (300–74; note in particular 337–9).

See especially Clay (1989: 17–94); concerning the meaning of *hubris*, see the entry in *The Oxford Classical Dictionary* (Hornblower and Spawforth 1996: 732–3).

77 *the many-footed beasts*: 'the many-footed' is a Greek kenning for the octopus.

80–1 *A most beautiful shrine as an oracle sought by humans*: Delos was famous as Apollo's birthplace, but the god's oracle on the island was obscure, in contrast to Delphi.

82 *Over all humans, since he will be known by many a name*: a lacuna is marked between this and the previous verse due to their apparent lack of continuity.

Delos is happy for Apollo to construct temples elsewhere and spread his worship 'over all humans', once he has built his first shrine upon her; by having many centres of worship he will come to be 'known by many a name'—names such as *Pytheios* (373), *Telphousios* (386), and *Delphinios* (495). In this respect the 'Pythian' section fulfils a prediction made in the 'Delian', a fact favouring the unity of the poem; however, the very proliferation of aetiology in the 'Pythian', contrasting with its absence from the 'Delian', has been used to impugn the integrity of the hymn.

85–6 *And the down-dripping water of Styx . . . Greatest and most dread oath*: concerning the significance of the oath sworn by the water of Styx see note on *Hy.* 4. 519.

91–2 *by pangs that offered no hope*: Leto cannot give birth in the absence of Eileithyia, goddess of childbirth, whom Hera is detaining on Olympos. Hera is jealous, not merely because her husband Zeus has slept with Leto and begotten offspring by her, but because this child will be 'a blameless and mighty son' (100), in contrast to Hera's, the lame Hephaistos (316–21). Hera retards the birth of Herakles too (*Iliad* 19. 95–133).

117–19 *She embraced the palm with her arms . . . and every goddess exclaimed*: Leto gives birth kneeling down, a common birth-posture in ancient Greece; the palm-tree against which she leans (mentioned at 18 above) was famous, featuring much in art and literature, and was supposed to be still preserved on the island in Roman times.

124 *Themis*: concerning the significance of Themis' role here see note on 67.

127–32 *But when, Phoibos, you had consumed . . . the unerring counsel of Zeus*: Apollo's miraculous infancy is paralleled by Demophoon's (*Hy.* 2. 231–41) and Hermes' (*Hy.* 4. 17–19; 409–14). In his first utterance the precocious god lays claim to two items closely associated with him, the lyre (which he plays at 515 below) and the bow (with which he slays the Snake at 357–8 below); he also marks out prophecy as his territory, in which he will act as mediator of the will of Zeus to humans (see note on 67). In the question of the hymn's unity it may be significant that here in the 'Delian' section two of Apollo's possessions are mentioned that feature in the 'Pythian', as also is prophecy, possibly foreshadowing the foundation described in the 'Pythian' section of Apollo's most famous oracle, that at Delphi. However, the lyre and bow are always likely to feature in any depiction of this deity, and the reference to prophecy may be simply following up the mention (at 80–1 above) of the oracle on Delos.

140–64   *But you whose bow is silver . . . singing matches so*: the poet shifts from myth to contemporary reality and to the festival held on Delos in Apollo's honour by the Ionians. At some point subsequent to the composition of this passage the festival went into decline, but Thucydides (3. 104), who quotes from our hymn, tells us that in 426–425 BC the Athenians reinstituted it, celebrating it every fourth year.

The natural assumption from this passage—that the hymn was first recited at this Delian festival—is one of the main arguments brought against the poem's unity, because it is thought improbable that a hymnist at this festival would go on to celebrate Apollo's oracle at Delphi at even greater length, and without once mentioning Delos after 181.

143–8   *Many shrines and wooded groves . . . of reverence, gather for you*: a priamel. See note on *Hy.* 1. 1–9.

158–61   *When they hymn first Apollo, and Leto . . . And charm the tribes of humans*: the Delian maidens are said to celebrate the gods first, and then to sing of 'the men and women of old': this corresponds to the notion that the *Hymns* themselves were preludes to longer recitations on heroic themes (see note on *Hy.* 2. 495).

162–4   *They know how to mimic the speech . . . singing matches so*: the Delian maidens are able to sing flawlessly in the various Greek dialects—and perhaps in 'barbarian' (i.e. non-Greek) languages also, represented by 'the babble' of 162 (though if another manuscript reading is adopted, the poet is claiming that they can imitate the sound of castanets).

165–76   *But come now, may Apollo . . . since it will indeed be the truth*: the poet refers to himself as a blind inhabitant of Khios, and Thucydides (3. 104), quoting these verses, identifies him as Homer. Khios was indeed one of several places that claimed Homer as a native son, and the declaration by the hymnist that all his songs are 'supreme' confirms the intention to bring Homer to mind, the poet whom none can surpass. However, few would now accept that Homer is the immediate author of any of the *Hymns*. The poet's declaration of identity has been described as a 'pious fraud', marking the hymn as the work of one of the *Homeridai*, 'Sons of Homer', a guild of bards on Khios who claimed descent from their renowned predecessor and regarded his poetry as their inheritance (Janko 1982: 114–15).

Was Homer blind? His blindness is a persistent part of the biographical tradition, but may have no firmer basis than an assumption that Demodokos, the blind bard of the *Odyssey*'s eighth book, is a self-portrait.

168 *some stranger suffering trials*: Odysseus describes himself at *Odyssey* 7. 24 as 'a stranger suffering trials' when newly arrived amongst the Phaiekes (Phaeacians), and later finds consolatory pleasure in the poetical skill of Demodokos (see note on 165–76).

177–8 *But I will not cease to hymn*: advocates of the hymn's unity take this declaration literally; others see it as a concluding formula, comparing the common transitional verse, 'But I will call to my mind both you and another song' (see note on *Hy.* 2. 495).

182 *The son of glorious Leto*: this is where the 'Pythian' section begins. Some have marked the end of the 'Delian' section after 178, but 179–81, with their mention of Lykia, Meionie, Miletos, and Delos, 'are still in the Ionian sphere' (Janko 1982: 99).

189–93 *All the Muses with beautiful voices . . . or defence against old age*: these verses stand in striking, and perhaps deliberate, contrast to the description at 151–5 above of the Ionians, who could easily be mistaken for gods by an onlooker: see Miller (1986: 69) and Clay (1989: 55). The movement from a festive assembly of godlike Ionians to one of genuine deities brings us up short if we have become too complacent, forgetting our human frailty and divine supremacy. For other statements of the weakness and stupidity of mortals see *Hy.* 2. 147–8, 216–17, 256–8, and also *Hy.* 3. 532–3.

207–15 *How shall I sing a hymn of you . . . Apollo who shoot from afar?*: this is a truncated priamel, used as a transitional device (see note on *Hy.* 1. 1–9). The poet pretends to hesitate over a choice of theme before deciding which option he will develop (cf. 19–29 above). Here the choice is between Apollo's amours, in which he competes with mortal heroes for the affections of mortal women, and his foundation of the Delphic oracle. The poet, in his apparent struggle to cope with the 'embarrassment of riches' available to one who would praise Apollo, at once pleases the god and tantalizes the audience.

213 *On foot, on a car the other; yet he was Triops' match*: this verse seems to describe a duel involving someone on foot (Apollo?) and someone on a chariot (Triops?); the details are lost in a lacuna between this and the previous verse. Compare the circumstances of Laios' death at the hands of his son Oidipous (Sophocles, *Oidipous Tyrannos* 800–13).

216–99 *When you descended Olympos . . . to be famed for ever in song*: Apollo's search for an oracular site parallels Leto's for a place in which to give birth (30–88); within these searches, Apollo's dealings with Telphousa correspond structurally to Leto's with Delos, but also provide in their content a balanced contrast—Delos, despite a groundless fear of Apollo's violence, decides to help Leto, whereas Telphousa, having tried to deceive Apollo, suffers his violent retribution.

223 *a holy, green mountain*: this has been identified as Messapion, an eminence on the Greek mainland opposite Euboian Khalkis.

225–8 *And arrived at the seat of Thebes . . . but forest held all in its grasp*: the site of Thebes, one of the greatest Greek cities, is an uninhabited wilderness when Apollo passes through it. For various interpretations of these verses see Janko (1986: 46), Miller (1986: 75), and Clay (1989: 58–9).

229–38 *From there you went on further . . . of god then guards the car*: in a digression concerning Onkhestos, a town in Boiotia, a rite is described that involves horses and a chariot in the grove of Poseidon, god of horses. Some have seen this as evidence that the author of the hymn's 'Pythian' section was a Boiotian. The rite may have been part of a festival held at Onkhestos in Poseidon's honour; it may also have had some connection with the death of Klymenos (father of the Erginos mentioned below at 297) from violence done to him by a *charioteer* within Poseidon's sanctuary at Onkhestos (Pausanias 9. 37. 1–2; Apollodorus 2. 4. 11).

In the rite the driver, having directed the chariot into the grove, disembarks—not to ease the horses, but rather to free them from human control, the 'dominion' of 234. If the chariot crashes, it is left on the spot, the horses are tended, and prayers are made to the god. The implication of 238, 'and the doom of god then guards the car', seems to be that the wrecked vehicle will be abandoned in the grove by the human participants in the rite, and whatever happens to it thereafter will be deemed the will of Poseidon. (In the phrase 'the doom of god', i.e. 'the doom *sent by* god', 'doom' translates *moira*, which means literally 'portion', but often approximates to 'destiny', 'fate'. Cf. *Odyssey* 3. 269, 'But when the doom of the gods (*moira theon*) fettered her so as to be tamed . . .'.)

The rite is so set up that it becomes a lottery whether or not the chariot, the man-made construction that the animals are being forced to draw, remains unscathed while they are free of their driver's control within a space sacred to their divine master. The purpose of this may be to give Poseidon a controlled opportunity to vent his anger at our subjugation of his animals, so that he will then be content to let us use them safely for our own needs. The epithet 'new-tamed' (231) suggests that the rite may have specifically involved young horses at the transitional point in their lives, when they have just been broken in.

This rite has long stimulated interest and debate. According to another noteworthy view, it was a form of divination. See Deubner (1938: 275–7), Jeanmaire (1945: 74–7), Clay (1989: 59), and (for an opposing interpretation) Schachter (1976).

244 *Telphousa*: she is at once a spring and the goddess of this spring. Her name, which takes various forms (e.g. Tilphousa, Tilphossa), is linked to Mount Tilphossion (a spur of Mount Helikon in Boiotia), and at 382–3 below the hymn appears to explain the formation of this mountain. Telphousa is an older, weaker, isolated, and parochial goddess who has to yield way to the young, powerful, Panhellenic, Olympian god; but in her subordination to him she provides Apollo with one of his many titles, *Telphousios* (375–87).

See Fontenrose (1959: 366–74), Janko (1986: 54–5), Miller (1986: 76–80, 90–1), Clay (1989: 58–60, 72–3), and Schachter (1994: 60–2).

249 *hundredfold offerings*: i.e. hecatombs. See note on *Hy*. 1. 12.

264–5   *To view the well-made cars and the clatter of quick-footed steeds*: an
instance of zeugma—'cars' can be 'viewed', 'clatter' cannot.

278–9   *Phlegyai, violent men, | Who, paying no heed to Zeus*: it would not
be fitting for a god nurtured by Themis (124–5) to dwell
amongst violent men who have no regard for Zeus (see note
on 67). The Phlegyai are descended from Ares' son Phlegyas,
whose name is derived from *phlego*, 'I burn'. Having migrated
south from Thessaly to Phokis in central Greece, they
attacked Apollo's oracle at Delphi: all but a few of them
perished from the wrath of the god (Pausanias 9. 36. 2). See
Janko (1992: 85).

287–95   *In this place it is my plan . . . stretching without a break*: these
verses repeat 247–55. Such repetitions are characteristic of
an oral poetic tradition, and are the rule in the *Iliad* and
Odyssey.

300–74   *But there was near by a fair-flowing . . . had rotted the monster
away*: Apollo wants mortals to come thronging to Delphi
with their sacrificial offerings; he therefore slays the monstrous Snake that had been harming both humans and
their animals in the vicinity (302–4). (In the Greek text the
word rendered as 'Snake' is *drakaina*, the feminine form of
drakon, from which the English word *dragon* is derived.)
From the *rotting* of the Snake's body in the heat of the sun
the place is called *Pytho* and the god himself *Pytheios* (371–
4): *pythein* in Greek means 'to make rot'. The etymology
behind this story is probably incorrect, but the Greeks
found such explanations irresistible (see 375–87 and 493–6
below, and also *Hy.* 5. 198–9, *Hy.* 19. 47). The episode is
thematically relevant to the hymn as a whole, since the
Snake through her nursling Typhaon is opposed to the rule
of Zeus, whose counsel Apollo wishes to dispense to
humans through his oracle: see note on 67, and Fontenrose
(1959: 13–22).

308–9   *When Kronos' son had begotten renowned Athena within | His head*:
on Athena's birth see *Hy.* 28. 4–16 and ATHENA.

322–5[a]   *Relentless, subtle in Craft . . . Take care now lest I think up*:
Hera hits home with a bitter pun: 'subtle in Craft' in 322
(*poikilometa* in the Greek) and 'think up' in 322 and 325[a]
(*metiseai* and *metisom'* respectively in the Greek) allude to the
goddess Metis (Craft/Resource), whose swallowing by Zeus

led to the birth of Athena (Janko 1991: 12). Note also 'Craft-filled' (*metioentos*) at 344, and see ATHENA.

332 *cow-eyed*: this is one of Hera's standard epithets in Homeric poetry, and is perhaps meant to indicate that her eyes are beautifully large. (It is also applied to Euryphaëssa at *Hy.* 31. 2.)

343–8 *From this moment onward then . . . and took from her offerings joy*: Hera withdraws from divine society, as does Demeter in *Hy.* 2. The consequences of these goddesses' withdrawals are potentially disastrous for Zeus and the other Olympians—a famine that threatens to wipe out sacrificial offerings from humans in Demeter's case, and the birth of the monster Typhaon in Hera's (see notes on 67 and *Hy.* 2. 91–7).

391–9 *While revolving this matter he saw . . . their black ship's course was bound*: just when Apollo is wondering who to appoint as priests in his new shrine, he sees a shipload of Cretan merchants bound for Pylos, and chooses them. Why does he pick foreigners instead of the nearby natives of Krisa (445–7)? Perhaps simply because they would be more single-mindedly devoted to him; however, they also serve to undermine local claims to any right of exclusive control over the oracle (see note on 540–3 below). The reason why the foreigners are specifically Cretan is uncertain—though if a Homeric poet had to pick a far-off people of seafarers who are also Greek, the Cretans would be the likely choice (see note on *Hy.* 2. 123).

396 *From the bay-tree*: the bay (or laurel, as it is often called) was sacred to Apollo. When delivering the god's prophecies, the Pythia, the priestess at Delphi, is said to have shaken a bay-tree that grew within the shrine: this brings to mind Zeus' oracle at Dodona, where the god's response was communicated through the priest-interpreted rustling of oak-leaves. The Pythia is also said to have burnt bay-leaves together with barley meal on an altar in Apollo's temple, to have chewed bay-leaves before delivering the responses, and to have worn a garland made from them. In addition, the first temple built at Delphi is supposed to have been made of bay-tree wood.

See Allen, Halliday, and Sikes (1936: 254); the entry

under *Delphic oracle* in *The Oxford Classical Dictionary* (Horn-blower and Spawforth 1996: 445); and, concerning the curious omission from the hymn of any reference to the Pythia, Clay (1989: 75–9) and Janko (1991: 13).

412–13   *the thick-fleeced flocks Of the lordly Sun*: compare the cattle of the Sun in the *Odyssey* (12. 127–41, 260–402), and the 'deathless cattle . . . owned by the blessed gods' at *Hy*. 4. 71; flocks of the Sun feature also at Herodotus 9. 93–4. The gods are not deficient in any form of wealth enjoyed by humans.

421–9   *To Arene and lovely Argyphea . . . With Same and wooded Zakynthos*: these verses echo the section of the Catalogue of Ships that deals with the contingent from Pylos (*Iliad* 2. 591–602), and also Telemakhos' return from Pylos to Ithake (*Odyssey* 15. 295–300). The Homeric epics were probably known to the hymnist, though not necessarily in written form; his use of formulae and verses from them is not incompatible with oral composition.

443   *Amidst the precious tripods*: metal tripods (cauldrons supported by three legs) were a common form of offering to the gods. At Delphi Apollo's priestess sat upon a tripod within the shrine when delivering the god's prophecies, and other tripods stood at the front of the building. At *Hy*. 4. 179 tripods are among the valuables that Hermes threatens to steal from Delphi.

448–85   *But he bounded aloft from there . . . for ever, throughout all time*: Apollo, disguised as a young man, questions the Cretans, who are ignorant of where they are and why they have been brought there, before disclosing his identity and what he wants of them. This episode is strongly reminiscent of *Odyssey* 13. 221–310, where Athena, appearing as a young herdsman to Odysseus, who has at last returned home but does not realize it, converses with him before revealing herself and her plans. Compare also the divine epiphanies to mortals at *Hy*. 2. 91–291, *Hy*. 5. 75–291, and *Hy*. 7. Apollo is trying to avoid frightening the Cretans by an overly abrupt declaration of himself and his purpose—at 462 he is said to 'put courage within their breasts'.

449–50   *in the shape of a fine strong man . . . whose locks about broad shoulders hung*: Dionysos takes on a similar appearance at

Hy. 7. 3–6. In their anonymous disguises the Homeric gods prefer forms that are youthful, strong, and beautiful.

452 *the liquid ways*: i.e. the sea; cf. *Hy.* 2. 43.

453–5 *or do you recklessly rove . . . Bringing harm to foreign nations?*: see note on *Hy.* 2. 125.

464–5 *Stranger—although in truth . . . but are like the immortal gods*: despite Apollo's disguise the Cretans' leader suspects that he may be dealing with a god; cf. *Hy.* 2. 159 and *Hy.* 5. 92–106. (I have followed here Miller 1986: 96.)

480 *I am the son of Zeus,* | *And my boast is that I am Apollo*: compare this declaration of identity with those of Demeter (*Hy.* 2. 268–9) and Dionysos (*Hy.* 7. 56–7). While Apollo's language is not modest, even mortals in Homeric epic boast of their lineage (e.g. *Iliad* 20. 200–41); if he wants humans' worship, he must make himself known to them in an impressive way.

493–6 *As at first in shape like a* dolphin *. . . be* Delphic *and present to view*: the poet correctly derives Apollo's title *Delphinios* from the Greek word for dolphin, *delphis*; he may also have derived, probably incorrectly, the name of Delphi itself from the same root, though he does not use this name in the hymn (in poetry *Pytho* is almost invariably preferred; *Hy.* 27. 14 is an exception to the rule). Seafarers would pray to Apollo Delphinios for protection, and would see his incarnation in the dolphin that played about their ship (Farnell 1896–1909: iv. 145).

The title given to the altar at 496 is problematic, as the manuscripts disagree at this point.

498 *And pour for the blessed gods*: i.e. make a libation (drink-offering) for them; so also at 512 below.

502–24 *When he had in this way spoken . . . the spirit was stirred in their breasts*: within this passage the poet, describing how the Cretans carry out Apollo's instructions, repeats almost verbatim most of 487–501 (excluding 493–6). Such repetitions, typical of Homeric poetry, are symptomatic of an oral poetic tradition. See note on 287–95.

529–30 *The land here, though lovely indeed . . . and attend to humans' needs*: The site chosen by Apollo for his oracle is barren, like his birthplace Delos (53–5); the Cretans will rely for sustenance on the offerings brought for the god. See Miller (1986: 105–7).

532–3 *You senseless humans, you wretched . . . For sorrows, hard toils, and troubles!*: for divine expressions of contempt at human stupidity see note on 189–93.

539–40 *in search, | Above all, of my guidance; but if*: the Greek text at this point seems to be corrupt, and the sense is uncertain.

540–3 *but if there will be a rash word . . . for ever forced under their yoke*: if the Cretans misbehave, they will be ruled by others. This smacks of being an after-the-event prophecy reflecting a conflict over control of the oracle in which its original operators lost out; it has been used to date the 'Pythian' section of the hymn to *c.*595–585 BC, the period in which the First Sacred War took place. In this struggle the town near Delphi called Krisa was destroyed, and its plain was seized and reserved for the god's flocks. The people of Krisa had tried to control the oracle, levying taxes on those who came to consult it; this led to military intervention by an amphictiony, a religious coalition of many Greek states, which subsequently oversaw the oracle's administration. To mark this victory over Krisa, the Pythian Games, originally celebrated every eight years and consisting solely of a hymnic contest in honour of Apollo, were set up in 582 BC on a grander scale, with the addition of athletic and other competitions, to be held every four years thereafter. The hymnic contest at the Pythian Games would have provided a suitable context for the first performance of the hymn's 'Pythian' section.

See Janko (1982: 119–21), and the entries under *amphictiony*, *Crisa*, *Pythian Games*, and *Sacred Wars* in *The Oxford Classical Dictionary* (Hornblower and Spawforth 1996: 75, 409, 1285, 1343–4); for a sceptical view, see Clay (1989: 87–90).

541 *outrageous conduct*: in the Greek text this is *hubris*; see note on 67.

544 *To you now all has been spoken; keep it safe in your thoughts*: for a similar admonition to a mortal to heed divine instructions see *Hy.* 5. 289–90.

546 *But I will call to my mind both you and another song*: see note on *Hy.* 2. 495.

Hymn 4: To Hermes

This is the latest of the long hymns, according to linguistic and stylistic analyses; it is usually dated towards the end of the sixth century BC. Latest in date, it is not least in merit, containing a well-knit plot and the *Hymns'* most appealing characterization—Hermes, the Trickster god, propelled by his inventive powers and humorous audacity from an obscure cave on Kyllene to Olympian splendour. It serves excellently as a companion-piece to *Hy.* 3, in which the new-born Apollo lays claim to the lyre and bow, and desires to pass on the will of Zeus to humans through prophecy (131–2): according to *Hy.* 4, Hermes invents the lyre and gives it to Apollo, may steal the latter's bow at some point in the future (see note on 519), and covets his Delphic oracle as a source of wealth (see notes on 173, 489). There are also narrative correspondences between the two poems—for example, both gods journey southwards from Pieria (Apollo to Delphi, *Hy.* 3. 216–99; Hermes toward Pylos, *Hy.* 4. 68–104), and Onkhestos is prominent on the route of each (*Hy.* 3. 229–38; *Hy.* 4. 87–94). The poet of *Hy.* 4 may well have been familiar with *Hy.* 3. Given the prominence of prophecy in *Hy.* 4, and in particular the justification of Apollo's *modus operandi* at Delphi at 541–9, together with the fact that the Bee Maidens whom Apollo gives to Hermes live near Delphi ('down in Parnassos' fold', 555), it is possible that *Hy.* 4 was composed for recitation at Delphi (Janko 1982: 148–9). A connection with Olympia has also been suggested (see notes on 115–33, 123–6).

Sophocles, the famous Athenian tragic poet of the fifth century BC, used the story of Hermes' cattle-theft as the subject of a satyr play, *Ikhneutai* or *The Searchers*, substantial fragments of which have survived: see Lloyd-Jones (1996: 140–77).

> 4 *having joined in love with*: i.e. having had sexual intercourse with. The Greek verb that denotes this activity, *meignumi*, means literally to 'mix' or 'mingle'.

> 7 *at the milking-time of night*: in some of its occurrences elsewhere this phrase seems to denote the twilight of morning or evening; here, however, it appears to mean 'at the dead of night'.

> 8 *Hera*: the idea of Zeus sneaking off to Maia while his wife sleeps is comical, but Hera's jealous anger could be perilous for the offspring of Zeus' philandering (e.g. Herakles) as well as for his paramours (at *Hy.* 3. 89–119 she tries to prevent Leto from giving birth).

14 *a leader of dreams*: one of Hermes' functions was to act as *psychopompos*, to escort the souls of the dead to Hades, and at the end of the hymn (572–3) he is officially appointed as 'messenger to Hades'; in this guise he can be seen at *Hy*. 2. 334–85, conveying to Hades Zeus' command that Persephone be returned to Demeter. In the Homeric epics Sleep and Death are twin brothers (*Iliad* 16. 672); the shade of the dead and the dream-figure, the spectre that appears to sleepers in dreams, are described in similar terms (compare e.g. *Iliad* 2. 5–83 and 23. 62–107); and Hermes, while escorting the shades of the Suitors to Hades in the *Odyssey*, passes 'the Land of Dreams' (24. 12). Hence Hermes is fittingly the leader of dreams, those neighbours of the dead.

15 *who lies in ambush at gates*: as god of thieves Hermes might watch gates in order to be ready for an opportune moment in which to sneak through them (he easily smuggles Priam inside the Greek camp at *Iliad* 24. 333–469), or to ambush anyone who would approach or come out of them; but also, on the principle 'set a thief to catch a thief', Hermes could stand guard at gates and doorways against any breaches of security.

20 *from his mother's deathless limbs*: i.e. from between her legs at birth.

21 *the sacred winnowing-fan*: the winnowing-fan, an instrument linked to both fertility and purification, serves as Hermes' cradle. If it was used for this purpose in real life, what was the intention behind the practice? Perhaps the child's growth is supposed to augment the harvest, or the harvest's fertility to rub off on the child and bring him good fortune; or perhaps the placing of the new-born infant in the winnowing-fan is intended to purify him of the pollution of birth. See Harrison (1903: 294–6, 315–17), Burkert (1985: 76), and the entries under *childbirth*, *pollution*, and *purification* in *The Oxford Classical Dictionary* (Hornblower and Spawforth 1996: 321, 1208–9, 1280).

26–7 *At the courtyard gates she met him, grazing in front of the house*: Maia lives in a cave on Mount Kyllene, but this is no bleak hole in the rock: as revealed here, it possesses a courtyard and gates, and can be called a 'house'; we learn later

(246–51) that it is also full of treasure. (Note 'she': the tortoise is feminine, as usual in Greek.)

30 *a sign of great profit*: Hermes, god of luck, chances upon the first *hermaion*—a lucky find, named after Hermes, who was thought to send it to the finder. Any such object that one stumbled across immediately on leaving the house would have extra significance.

31–2 *Hello there, shapely charmer . . . who come most welcome to view!*: Hermes addresses the tortoise as if she has already become the lyre, seeing beyond her present waddling ugliness.

36 *It is better to be at home,* ¹*Since harm lies out of doors*: this is the most obvious translation of the Greek verse, but in Hesiod it recurs with a different meaning: 'It is better ⟨for things⟩ to be at home, since what is outside is at risk' (*Works and Days* 365; see West 1978: 248). Hermes may be cleverly using the same words both to reassure the tortoise that she will be safer inside the cave than outside and to tell himself that he must bring his new possession inside in order not to lose it. Of course, within the cave the tortoise will find death rather than freedom from harm, when her flesh is parted from the safe home of her shell.

37 *baneful spells*: see *Hy.* 2. 227–30 for another reference to magic in the *Hymns*. According to one source the living tortoise can act as a charm against hail; the dead animal had commoner magical uses (Allen, Halliday, and Sikes 1936: 282–3).

41–51 *There tossing her up, with a knife . . . to serve as harmonious strings*: from the shell of the tortoise Hermes invents the seven-stringed lyre, which later proves crucial to the plot (418–502). According to other sources, the seven-stringed lyre was invented by Terpander, a poet active in Sparta in the early seventh century BC; the commonest older form of the instrument had four strings. See Càssola (1975: 166–70), and the entry under *music* in *The Oxford Classical Dictionary* (Hornblower and Spawforth 1996: 1004–5).

50 *the yoke*: i.e. the bridge of the instrument.

68–9 *the Sun . . . with horses and car*: concerning the Sun's horses and chariot see note on *Hy.* 31. 14.

71 *deathless cattle . . . owned by the blessed gods*: see note on *Hy.* 3.

412–13. These cattle are called 'deathless', even though Hermes later kills two of them (116–20): 'deathless' here must mean either 'immune to death from natural causes' or (more probably) 'belonging to the deathless gods'.

75–86 *Turning aside their steps . . . as making speed a long journey*: on the sandy ground Hermes drives the cattle backwards by a convoluted route while walking backwards himself: clearly his purpose is to confuse pursuers with a misleading trail. He then improvises a pair of sandals, the tracks of which will later baffle Apollo (219–26, 346–9). Presumably Hermes makes them with that end in view, and also to allow himself a forward gait; but the poet does not spell this out. The phrase 'avoiding the walk ¹From Pieria' (85) suggests that Hermes gains as much in comfort as he does in stealth from his new footwear—and note what he later hopes will be the clinching point in his denial of the cattle-theft: 'soft are my feet, and rough underfoot is the ground' (273). Textual corruption at the end of 86 prevents certainty of interpretation. Sandals are, of course, a fitting invention for the god of travellers.

As messenger of the gods Hermes acquires a pair of golden sandals that transport him quickly over both land and sea (*Odyssey* 5. 44–6). His sandals in the hymn seem not to have any such magical properties.

88 *Onkhestos*: other versions of the story place the witnessing of the theft in the Peloponnesos. There is no obvious reason why the hymnist should choose this Boiotian town—a centre of Poseidon's worship, not Hermes'—as the home of the Old Man, unless he is himself Boiotian and/or is showing familiarity with *Hy.* 3. 229–38, where Apollo passes through Onkhestos on his way to Delphi.

91–3 *Wine will be yours in plenty . . . suffer no harm at all*: Hermes predicts a rich harvest for the Old Man, and then urges him to keep quiet about what he has seen: the god does not coarsely spell out the implied link between the Old Man's silence and his future prosperity. But despite subsequently giving information to Apollo (202–11), the Old Man simply disappears from the poem after a passing reference in Apollo's speech to Zeus (354–5). In other versions—one of which may derive from Hesiod—the human witness (called

Battos) demands a reward as the price of his silence, to
which Hermes agrees; the god returns in disguise to test the
man's fidelity with a bribe, and he succumbs to temptation;
Hermes punishes him by turning him to stone. See Evelyn-
White (1914: 262–7).

109 *He seized and stripped with iron a bay-tree's splendid bough*: a
lacuna is marked after this verse because the extant text
refers only to the preparatory stripping of a single fire-stick,
when two are needed to kindle fire through friction-
generated heat.

111 *Hermes it was who first discovered fire-sticks and fire*: Hermes is
the first to produce fire with fire-sticks; he does not invent
fire itself, which is the property of Hephaistos ('While the
might of renowned Hephaistos kindled the flames . . .', 115).
Yet while Hermes devises this fire-kindling technique, he is
not said to pass it on to humans, although it does eventually
reach us, like the lyre: his inventions are first and foremost
for himself, and only secondarily benefit others. If humans
have fire, that is because the wily Titan Prometheus stole it
for us from heaven in a hollow fennel stalk against the will of
Zeus (Hesiod, *Theogony* 562–9). Prometheus and Hermes
are both examples (the former more beneficent than the
latter) of a figure seen in many cultures, the Trickster, who is
cunning, mischievous, inventive, and ambivalent in character, sometimes a blessing to humanity, sometimes a curse
(see 576–8 below). Radin (1956) offers a non-Classical
example.

115–33 *While the might of renowned Hephaistos . . . The meat down his
sacred throat*: Hermes' butchery of two cattle again recalls
Prometheus, who was responsible for the division of the
sacrificial victim between gods and humans (Hesiod,
Theogony 535–61). Hermes becomes the god of heralds
and the herald of the gods: Zeus, on first seeing his son,
remarks that he 'has about him a herald's look' (331).
Homeric heralds are concerned not just with bearing messages and making proclamations, but also with the conduct
of sacrifices and feasting (Heubeck, West, and Hainsworth
1988: 89–90); Hermes' invention of an equitable way of
dividing and distributing meat may therefore be linked with
his future role as divine herald. His division of the meat into

twelve portions (128) seems likely to refer to the Twelve Olympians (who are—if Hestia is excluded—Zeus, Hera, Poseidon, Demeter, Ares, Hephaistos, Aphrodite, Athena, Apollo, Artemis, Dionysos, and Hermes himself). The fact that the portions are to be allocated by lot (129) implies equality between their intended recipients; if these are the Twelve Olympians, Hermes, by setting aside distinctions of seniority and power, is signalling that he wants to enter into their company on an equal basis (Clay 1989: 121–2).

Another view, according to which Hermes is establishing a local rite that required a twelvefold sacrificial division, connects the hymn with the Cult of the Twelve Gods at Olympia. This town, where the Olympic Games were held, stood beside the river Alpheios, which is near the scene of Hermes' activities (101, 139, 398). The Twelve Gods were divided into pairs, each pair sharing an altar: Zeus–Poseidon, Hera–Athena, Hermes–Apollo, the Graces–Dionysos, Artemis–Alpheios, Kronos–Rhea. The importance of Apollo in the hymn might reflect his sharing of an altar with Hermes in this cult; there are, however, problems, most notably that in other sources the cult at Olympia was established by Herakles (see Pindar, *Olympian Odes* 5. 5–6; 10. 24–59).

Hermes' abstention from eating the meat despite its tempting smell (130–3) may be intended to emphasize his divine status: the gods do not normally eat meat, contenting themselves with nektar and ambrosia, supplemented by the odour and steam of their burnt share of the sacrifice. But possibly it is designed to explain why a mortal celebrant performing a sacrifice modelled on that of Hermes did not eat any meat himself.

For different interpretations of this difficult passage see Burkert (1984) and Clay (1989: 116–27).

122 *The chines of honour's share*: the chine was the most coveted portion of the animal, and its bestowal showed the recipient's honoured position in the community.

123–6 *While these on the ground were lying . . . and will unceasingly be*: these verses may refer to a specific cult centre by the river Alpheios where there was a cave with either stone outcroppings shaped like oxhides or a pair of actual, antique oxhides—Radermacher (1931: 95–6) compares the skin of Marsyas (Herodotus 7. 26; Xenophon, *Anabasis* 1. 2. 8). Yet there is a puzzling vagueness concerning the location of this cave. Pylos is mentioned (216, 342, 355, 398), but it is not clear how close this town is to the cave, and even in antiquity there was dispute over where Homeric Pylos was (see PYLOS). By stressing the hides' endurance in front of the cave, the poet distracts attention from Hermes' uncharacteristic, but necessary, negligence: a token of the butchery has to be left exposed for Apollo's subsequent enlightenment and to precipitate the crisis of the poem (403–8).

134–41 *He set down in the high-roofed byre . . . in Selene's beautiful light*: this passage presents difficulties. At 134–6 it is not clear why Hermes 'raises aloft' the meat that he has just 'set down' in the cave. Is he trying to conceal incriminating evidence, or is he erecting a trophy to commemorate his cattle-theft? Also difficult is the elimination of the traces of the fire. Hermes is here described as spending 'all the night' (141) on this process, but above (97–100) he arrives beside Alpheios as morning approaches. Later it appears as if his cleaning-up of the fire was not as thorough as it might have been (see note on 415).

145 *and not a dog had barked*: the god of thieves has special powers with which to get past all the usual obstacles to theft, including dogs; one of his commonest titles, *Argeiphontes* (understood in ancient times as 'Slayer of Argos'), may originally have meant 'Dog-Killer'. See West (1978: 368–9).

156 *parading your barefaced cheek*: literally, 'clothed in shamelessness'.

163 *why aim this abuse at me*: the sense here is uncertain, as the Greek text at this point is perhaps corrupt.

173 *that rite which Apollo enjoys*: the rite in question is prophecy, which brings wealth, and hence 'honour' in the Homeric, material sense, to Apollo at his Delphic oracle.

213–14 *He was watching a long-winged bird . . . was the son of Kronos' son Zeus*: Apollo, god of prophecy, discovers the thief's identity by suitably ominous means: the cries and flight of birds were viewed as omens conveying messages to those skilled in reading them (see 541–9). It is important that Apollo does not find the thief by seeing through Hermes' precautions against pursuit: the god of thieves must not lose face through any lack of skill in his first theft. In fact, this mantic short-cut brings the thief renown, as his marvellous exploit—which otherwise would have been unknown or at best anonymous— is recounted to the Olympian gods by the indignant Apollo (334–64).

218 *The Far-shooter noticed the tracks*: at 75–88 the sandy region on which Hermes and the cattle leave their tracks lies between Pieria and Onkhestos; here Apollo notices the tracks after leaving Onkhestos; at 340–55 Apollo, recounting events for Zeus, mentions the tracks *before* referring to the mortal witness of the theft, implying that he had followed the trail as far as Onkhestos, where he lost it, but then had the Old Man's report to guide him. This is not a discrepancy likely to trouble an audience, and the poet probably wished to juxtapose Apollo's speech of wonder at the tracks with his meeting with the god who made them.

221 *the asphodel meadow*: in the *Odyssey* there is an asphodel meadow in the land of the dead (11. 539); the asphodel plant, however, is real rather than mythical, and there are no underworld connotations here, since the meadow to which Apollo refers is in Pieria, near Olympos.

222–6 *But these are steps | That belong . . . these here are stranger still*: Apollo's bewilderment over who could have made the second set of tracks underlines Hermes' status. He is no human, animal, or Centaur: he is a god.

242 *the tortoise-lyre*: the poet is careful to mention the lyre here, lest we forget about it entirely; it disappears now until 418, when Hermes uses it to win over Apollo. If we press the poet hard, he will have to admit that the infant god carries it under his arm, without exciting Apollo's curiosity, from Kyllene to Olympos and then to the cave where the cattle are hidden. Plausibility is sacrificed to narrative economy, with small loss; the very suddenness of the lyre's reappearance at 418 helps us share in Apollo's wonder.

259 *and will rule amongst the little men*: who these 'little men' are is uncertain: perhaps the dead in general, imagined as being diminished in size; or perhaps the shades of dead children, fitting subjects for the infant Hermes to rule.

263–4 *Not a sight did I see, not a fact . . . collect | An informer's fee*:

Hermes adopts precisely the course that he urged the Old Man to follow (92–3).

265–73 *I don't even look like a mighty man . . . and rough underfoot is the ground*: Hermes uses arguments from probability in denying the theft. The picture of the guilty infant employing law-court sophistry would have appealed greatly to an ancient audience; the fact that much of the humour of the hymn depends upon Hermes' verbal dexterity has prompted the suggestion that it was composed in the period when the rhetorical teachings of the Sophists came into vogue in the fifth century BC. However, the Greeks always took delight in verbal evasions and trickery, as the figure of Odysseus in the *Odyssey* shows.

274–7 *Yet by my father's head . . . this rumour is all that I hear*: Hermes rounds off his oration with an oath which both draws attention to his identity ('by *my father's* head') and brings to a fitting climax his masterful display of prevarication ('I neither declare myself to be guilty . . .' is not quite the same as 'I am not guilty').

294–303 *But the mighty Slayer of Argos . . . moreover, will lead the way*: the 'brazen labouring man' (296) who comes from Hermes' belly is usually understood to be an emission of wind (either a fart or a belch), named in the manner of a kenning. A sneeze follows at once; Apollo puts down the child, but claims that 'by means of these omens' (303) he will find his cattle, with Hermes leading the way. As it turns out, Apollo does recover his animals (or at least all but two of them), and Hermes does lead the way, though the command of Zeus rather than these omens is what is immediately responsible (391–400).

The sneeze, due to its involuntary and startling nature, was held to be a genuine omen, either confirming words or actions just spoken or completed, or else having a checking force, signalling that some action should *not* be attempted (see *Odyssey* 17. 539–47; Xenophon, *Anabasis* 3. 2. 9; Aristotle, *Problems* 962[b]19–28). It seems likely, however, that the emission of wind is a parodic omen—but a parody of what? The sneeze itself, or a peal of thunder, are the most obvious possibilities. Another is ventriloquism ('belly-talking'), familiar in Greece as a form of prophecy by at least the fifth century BC (see Aristophanes, *Wasps* 1017–22).

Perhaps Hermes imbues both omens with a checking force, compelling Apollo to stop laying hands on him (note 'though eager to speed on the way', 299), and Apollo (the god of prophecy *par excellence*) then turns the tables on him by interpreting them as omens of confirmation; or perhaps Hermes *intends* them to be taken as genuine, involuntary omens of confirmation, hoping to distract Apollo from his present violence.

314 *the shepherd Hermes*: Hermes' native place, Arkadia, was a region abundant in sheep (there are sheep grazing about Maia's cave at 232), and the god was thought to have much power in the agricultural sphere; near the end of the hymn (570) he gains official control over sheep as well as over other animals.

325 *. . . held snowy Olympos*: what it is that 'holds' Olympos here is uncertain, as the Greek text seems to be corrupt at this point.

331 *who has about him a herald's look*: see note on 115–33.

372 *and brought no blessed gods\As witnesses or observers*: comically, the guilty thief complains about the non-observance of legal niceties—the criminal, as ever, sheltering behind the technicalities of the law. Hermes' point is that, when a house is searched for stolen property, witnesses should be brought who can later swear that what the searcher claims to have found there was in fact found there, and that nothing was planted or abstracted (cf. Plato, *Laws* 954a–c).

379–80 *May I be blessed so sure . . . And I'm telling the perfect truth*: another example of Hermes' casuistic skill. He did not drive the cattle home, but rather to the cave by the Alpheios river; he did in fact cross the threshold when he first set out (23), but perhaps he, the audience, and poet alike have forgotten this, remembering only the manner of the god's return— through the equivalent of the keyhole (145–7).

381–6 *I have great respect for the Sun . . . let you give the younger your help*: common elements of Homeric oaths are (i) the invocation of deities such as Zeus, Earth, and Sun as witnesses; (ii) the touching or naming of potent objects, such as Zeus' head (see note on 274–7) or the water of Styx (see note on 519);

(iii) the statement of the oath's subject-matter; and (iv) a call for the swearer to be punished if guilty of perjury or oath-breaking. (See *Iliad* 19. 257–65; Burkert 1985: 250–4.) The cunning Hermes calls nobody to witness the truth of what he says, merely professing 'great respect' (381) for the Sun in particular—so healthy is this respect that he commits the theft by night, so that the Sun can know nothing about it. Then, coming to the matter in dispute, he states elliptically that he is not guilty, but without specifying within the oath what he is not guilty of. This reticence allows him to swear with confidence (and bathos) 'by this well-adorned Front door of immortals!' (384)—the very entrance through which he wishes to enter (by stealth, one suspects, if no invitation is forthcoming), and the very space that he will later protect (see note on 15 above). Finally, instead of inviting punishment on himself if he has sworn falsely, Hermes threatens vengeance against Apollo.

386 *let you give the younger your help*: Hermes ends with a shrewd appeal for his father's sympathy: Zeus himself is a youngest son, and overthrew his father Kronos and the other Titans (see KRONOS).

388 *And he kept without casting aside the swaddling-bands on his arm*: to cast aside the swaddling-bands would be to cast aside the rhetorically useful appearance of infancy. The incongruity of such a speech coming from an infant's lips is what provokes the mirth that saves Hermes from punishment.

392 *And instructed Conductor Hermes to lead the way*: 'Conductor' is perhaps how the poet understood *diaktoros*, one of Hermes' commonest epithets, and his intention here may be to explain its origin.

409–14 *He spoke these words and started . . . While Apollo looked on with wonder*: Maia predicted that Apollo would put about her son's ribs 'bonds that nothing can loose' (157), but Hermes proves her wrong. Not only do the bonds fail to hold him, but under his control they grow over the cattle, which he clearly wants to keep. The failure of an attempted fettering is a feature of Dionysos' epiphany at *Hy.* 7. 12–14 (compare also in that hymn the spreading of a vine and ivy over the pirates' ship, 38–42); and at *Hy.* 3. 127–9 the new-born

Apollo himself cannot be held by bonds once he has tasted nektar and ambrosia.

415   *the gleaming fire*: since Hermes had earlier obliterated all traces of the fire (140–1), it is hard to see why he should be worried about it now. Perhaps a verse has dropped out of the Greek text, taking with it the true object of 'hide' in 416.

427   *bringing to pass*: see note on 559.

430   *for she was assigned Maia's son*: Mnemosyne, 'Memory', is a goddess vital to the poet, for without her he cannot function; hence she is the Muses' mother. Hermes' musical and verbal talents mark him out as, in a sense, her subject.

448   *The beaten track*: possibly a metaphorical term for the practice that will lead to skilful playing on the lyre; but cf. 'the splendid path of song' at 451 below.

461   *I'll seat . . . as Guide*: the Greek text here seems to be corrupt, and the sense is uncertain.

473   *Now in these I've learnt myself | That you, my boy, are rich*: again the Greek text seems to be corrupt, and the sense is uncertain.

482–8   *When one who has learned the knowledge . . . A pointless, high-pitched jangle*: Hermes presents the lyre as if it is an oracle that will yield the desired response only if 'questioned' correctly (cf. below 543–9 and 558–66).

489   *but you can freely choose | To learn whatever you wish*: this statement is repeated from 474, and signifies here that Apollo will not be clumsy in 'putting questions' to the lyre. But Hermes' harping upon Apollo's ability to learn 'whatever you wish' hints that he (Hermes) would like to learn something (i.e. prophecy) too.

511–12   *But Hermes sought out for himself . . . that can far away be heard*: this brief, final demonstration of Hermes' inventiveness compensates him for his loss of the lyre with another musical instrument, and—in view of 496–9—one which is apt, since it was an instrument favoured by herdsmen. The syrinx was associated also with Hermes' son Pan (see *Hy.* 19. 15), and is better known today as the 'pan-pipes'.

516   *acts of barter*: a euphemism for theft, which commerce is often thought to resemble. Hermes was in fact god of merchants as well as of thieves. In Ovid's *Fasti* (5. 681–92), when a

merchant prays to Mercury (the Roman Hermes) to be
excused past and future perjury, the god laughs, remembering his own cattle-theft.

519 *by either nodding your head Or making your vow upon the potent*
water of Styx: nodding down was a gesture of assent (nodding
up signalled dissent). In the *Iliad* (1. 514–30) Zeus says that
his nod is 'the greatest token amongst the immortals', and
that it is 'not revocable, deceptive, or without fulfilment';
when he does nod, all Olympos shakes (see *Hy.* 1. 13–16).
The Stygian oath, sworn by the water of the river Styx in the
underworld, is described by Hesiod (*Theogony* 775–806): to
settle a dispute on Olympos, Zeus has a jug of the water of
Styx brought and the god taking the oath pours a libation
from it; if he swears falsely, he falls into a year-long coma (as
near to death as a god can come), followed by a nine-year
exile from the other gods. Apollo is perhaps guilty of
stupidity in allowing Hermes to nod assent instead of
insisting upon the Stygian oath, for Hermes' nod may not
be quite as irrevocable as that of Zeus. In some traditions he
does steal Apollo's bow.

526 *And out a perfect*: more than one verse seems to have been lost
after these words; in the next surviving verse Apollo is
speaking directly.

529 *a beautiful rod*: this is one of Hermes' traditional accoutre-
ments, with which he can put to sleep or wake up whomso-
ever he desires. He employs it in smuggling Priam into the
Greek camp (*Iliad* 24. 343–5), and in conducting the shades
of the slain Suitors to Hades (*Odyssey* 24. 2–5).

552–63 *For certain holy virgins . . . amongst one another and lie*: Hermes
had been casting a greedy eye on Apollo's Delphic oracle
(see 172–81); Apollo fobs him off with three bee-like
nymphs who prophesy outside of the Zeus–Apollo mantic
conduit. Their honeycomb diet may hint at the use of
fermented honey (mead) as an intoxicating tool to induce
a state of prophetic inspiration. Honey is frequently associated with poetry as well as with prophecy, and the Greeks
regarded both as being the result of divine inspiration.
Prophetic responses were given in verse, and Apollo was
no less a god of music and poetry than he was of prophecy.
See Scheinberg (1979), though contrast Larson (1995).

554　*They have white barley bestrewn | On their heads*: this barley has been compared to the pollen that commonly adheres to bees.

559　*and bring all things to pass*: the power to predict events through prophecy merges with the idea of actually causing them. The same verb is used at 427, where Hermes, by singing of the origin of the gods and Earth, brings them into being once more; the music that he creates and the prophecy that he covets are presented as analogous (see notes on 482–8, 552–63).

562　*the gods' | Sweet food*: usually nektar and ambrosia are the gods' food.

569–73　*And that over bright-eyed lions . . . give not the smallest share*: the end of Apollo's speech is missing, and also the main clause governing 569–73. Probably, when Apollo finished speaking, Zeus added to the blessings that Hermes had already received. Hermes' appointment as messenger to Hades (572–3; see note on 14) would certainly seem to be in the gift of Zeus alone. The reference to Hades is itself cryptically phrased: presumably the honour that the miserly lord of the dead will give is that of accepting Hermes as Zeus' messenger.

576–8　*With all mortals and immortals both . . . the tribes of mortal men*: see note on 111.

580　*But I will call to my mind both you and another song*: see note on *Hy.* 2. 495.

Hymn 5: To Aphrodite

This poem is held by many to be the oldest and most 'Homeric' of the *Hymns*; it has been dated to *c.*675–660 BC (Janko 1982: 200). In it Zeus makes Aphrodite fall in love with the mortal Ankhises, in order to put an end to her mockery of the other gods, who at her contriving have had similar degrading dalliances with humans (45–55); Aphrodite seduces Ankhises and conceives their son, Aineias (see note on 198–9). In so far as it shows one god tricking another, it calls to mind the 'Lay of Demodokos' (*Odyssey* 8. 266–366), in which Hephaistos snares his wife Aphrodite and her lover Ares in bed together. However, Demodokos' song is confined purely to the divine realm, whereas the hymn shows the divine manifesting itself in the mortal sphere and having a beneficial, enriching effect, embodied in the hero Aineias. The hymn

also contains echoes of another epic passage, the 'Deception of Zeus'
(*Iliad* 14. 153–353), in which Hera, decking herself out alluringly,
seduces Zeus in order to distract his attention from the fighting at
Troy; again, in contrast to the hymn, the action in this episode is
confined to the divine realm, though its consequences do affect the
warring Greeks and Trojans.

Some have argued that the hymn is the work of the same poet—
Homer?—who composed *Iliad* 20. 75–352, where Aineias confronts
Akhilleus; it has also been contended that this poet is aiming to please
the Aineiadai, a royal family claiming descent from Aineias and ruling
near the site of Troy (see note on 196–7). It would be gratifying if at
least one of the *Hymns* could be attributed with confidence to Homer,
but in recent times doubts have been cast not just on the hymn's
connection with the *Iliad*, but also on the connection of both hymn and
epic with the Aineiadai: see Edwards (1991: 298–301).

7–44   *There are three whose minds she cannot . . . his revered and true-*
       hearted wife: the poet, before launching into the main body of
       his hymn, celebrates in three miniature hymns the god-
       desses immune to Aphrodite's manipulation: Athena, Arte-
       mis, and Hestia. (No male deity can resist her.) By counting
       off on the fingers of one hand, so to speak, those free of her
       influence, the hymnist illustrates the extent of her power. In
       addition, 40–4 could constitute a hymn in honour of Hera:
       her unsurpassable excellence as a wife is stressed to high-
       light Aphrodite's ability to make even Zeus himself unfaith-
       ful with lowly mortal women.

16   *with distaff of gold, whose cry resounds*: see note on *Hy.* 27. 1.

19   *piercing cries*: the word for 'cry' in the Greek text here is the
       untranslatable *ololuge*, a ululation made usually by women,
       and more often to signal joy than sorrow.

23   *a second birth*: of the children of Kronos and Rhea Hestia was
       born first and regurgitated last (the regurgitation being the
       'second birth'), and so is both the eldest and the youngest of
       them. See KRONOS.

24   *Whom Poseidon wooed and Apollo*: the story of these wooings
       has not been preserved. That Poseidon, her brother, should
       want her as his wife is less surprising (given the marriage of
       their siblings Zeus and Hera) than that Apollo, her nephew,
       should desire her (an uncle marrying his niece is better

paralleled—e.g. Hades and Persephone). Hestia is Apollo's housekeeper at Delphi according to *Hy.* 24. 1–2.

29–32 *Father Zeus then gave . . . the eldest amongst the gods*: being not just goddess of the hearth but also the hearth itself, Hestia is present and honoured in every home and every temple. See *Hy.* 29. 1–6.

39 *joined him together with mortal women in love*: see note on *Hy.* 4. 4.

60–3 *There, having gone inside . . . which had been perfumed for her*: these verses echo *Iliad* 14. 169–72, where Hera prepares herself for her seduction of Zeus. It has been suggested that the oil which features in both passages is actually applied to the goddesses' garments rather than their skin: see Janko (1992: 174–5).

68 *the mother of beasts*: this phrase is applied to Mount Ida, not to Aphrodite. Compare *Hy.* 19. 30, 'Arkadia . . . where many fountains flow, The mother of flocks'.

80 *and was piercingly playing the lyre*: the embassy sent to persuade Akhilleus to return to battle similarly finds him playing the lyre and singing of 'the glorious deeds of men' (*Iliad* 9. 185–91); the lyre and song are not the exclusive preserve of the professional bard in Homeric poetry.

82 *a maiden as yet untamed*: see note on *Hy.* 17. 4.

92–106 *You are welcome, Queen, to this house . . . and reach the threshold of age*: despite Aphrodite's disguise, Ankhises immediately suspects that she is a goddess. Cf. *Hy.* 2. 159, *Hy.* 3. 464–5.

106 *the threshold of age*: an ambiguous phrase, denoting either the threshold which *is* old age (taken as an intermediate stage between life and death), or the threshold over which one crosses when entering old age at the end of one's vigorous maturity.

108–42 *Ankhises, greatest in glory . . . and immortal gods esteem*: Aphrodite's pretence that she is a Phrygian princess abducted by Hermes to be Ankhises' bride brings to mind both Demeter's false tale of abduction (*Hy.* 2. 119–44) and also the actual abduction of Persephone by Hades (*Hy.* 2. 2–39); compare too Apollo's deception of the Cretans (*Hy.* 3. 448–62).

113–16 *But I have perfect knowledge . . . of your people's language, at least*: the 'daughter of Otreus' explains how she can speak Trojan

in addition to her native Phrygian tongue; the fictitious
'Trojan nurse' is a plausible detail that cunningly buttresses
the story (Walcot 1991: 145). The apparent local knowledge
that these verses display has fuelled speculation that the
hymn originated in Asia Minor. In the *Iliad*, where the
Trojans and Phrygians are allies, no difference in language
between them is mentioned.

117–30   *But now the Slayer of Argos . . . and upon me was mighty
constraint*: Hermes is supposed to have snatched the 'daughter of Otreus' from a dance in honour of Artemis and to have
brought her to Ankhises. At *Iliad* 16. 179–92 Hermes
himself becomes enamoured of a mortal woman whom he
sees in Artemis' dance: the dance of the virgin goddess
would have been one of the few occasions when nubile
young Greek women congregated in public view (Janko
1992: 342–3). For a similar abduction by a god of one from
a group of maidens and a subsequent magical journey see
Hy. 2. 2–39, where Hades seizes Persephone from amongst
the daughters of Ocean.

118   *with distaff of gold, whose cry | Resounds*: see note on *Hy.* 27. 1.

119   *many nymphs | And cattle-yielding maidens*: it seems strange that
nymphs should be dancing with mortal women, even if the
human Phaiekes are visited by the gods without disguise
(*Odyssey* 7. 201–6); perhaps 'nymphs' here means 'brides' or
'young girls'. The expression 'cattle-yielding maidens'
implies that a suitor offered a price in the form of cattle
for a woman's hand in marriage (Edwards 1991: 229).

131–42   *But I beg you, by Zeus and your parents . . . and immortal gods
esteem*: the 'daughter of Otreus' seems to envisage that she
and Ankhises will wait until their families have been
informed and the nuptials properly celebrated before con-
summating their union; Aphrodite shows her skill in the art
of seduction by using a suggestion of delay to so inflame
Ankhises' desire that he will accept nothing short of instant
gratification (Clay 1989: 177–8). The incontinence that
leads him to breach human convention demonstrates the
power of the goddess, but is matched by her inability to keep
within divine social norms by not sleeping with a mortal (the
only truthful verse of her first speech to Ankhises is 130, 'But
here to you I came, and upon me was mighty constraint'). In

this situation appearance (a helpless maiden at the mercy of a man's uncontrollable lust) is the opposite of reality (a helpless man manipulated at will by a goddess, who is herself in the grip of a Zeus-inflicted infatuation).

140 *payment*: this is often interpreted as a dowry, but the Greek word here is *apoina*, which usually denotes a ransom or other payment made in compensation (at 210 below Zeus gives as *apoina* to Tros heavenly horses, to compensate for the loss of his son). Her parents must buy back the 'daughter of Otreus' from Ankhises before he can marry her in due form. See Keaney (1981) for analysis.

149–54 *then of gods and mortal men . . . to enter Hades' abode*: no god, let alone man, will stand in the way of Ankhises' passion. This overweening defiance, which again shows the power of sexual desire pushing its victim beyond the bounds of propriety, may foreshadow the subsequent disregard for the gods on the part of Ankhises that causes Zeus in some sources to strike him with the thunderbolt (see note on 281–90).

It is not surprising that Ankhises singles out Apollo as a possible divine opponent: not only is he the outstanding sender of sudden death to men (as his sister Artemis is to women), he is also in frequent rivalry with mortal men in affairs of the heart, not always successfully (see *Hy.* 3. 208–13).

157–60 *To the bed that was finely strewn . . . the hero himself had slain*: Ankhises' bed, though comfortable, shows evidence of his masculine prowess: he himself killed the bears and lions whose hides form part of it, a fact that diminishes any contempt towards him that his easy deception by the goddess might arouse. But these hides of bears and lions call to mind the wolves, lions, bears, and panthers that fawned on Aphrodite earlier and copulated under her influence (69–74): Ankhises turns out to be just as vulnerable to erotic desire as the predators who are his prey.

173–5 *Her head reached the well-wrought roof-beam . . . fair-crowned goddess belongs*: compare this transformation with Demeter's temporary epiphany at *Hy.* 2. 188–90, where there is an identical increase in size accompanied by a burst of light and

feelings of fear and awe in the human onlooker; note also
Hy. 2. 275–80, *Hy.* 3. 440–50.

181 *Aphrodite's neck and beautiful eyes*: in the *Iliad* (3. 396–7) Helen
recognizes the disguised Aphrodite by her 'beautiful neck,
lovely breasts, and sparkling eyes'.

187–90 *Yet by Zeus who bears the aigis . . . has no flourishing life*:
Ankhises fears a permanent debility, a post-coital lassitude
from which he will never recover (Clay 1989: 182–3); within
this fear will be the worry that his union with the goddess
may have used up all his procreative power to no effect—a
feature of the 'flourishing life' is 'offspring blooming with
health' (104). Aphrodite consoles him on this point with the
news that she will herself bear him a son, Aineias (196–9).

In most versions of the story Aineias is an only child; but
in the *Iliad* (13. 428–33) Ankhises and an unnamed wife are
said to have daughters (number unspecified), the eldest of
whom is called Hippodameia.

196–7 *You will have a son of your own . . . will never lack children
themselves*: Aineias is prominent in the *Iliad*, in which it is
predicted that he will survive the war at Troy and will rule
the Trojan people (20. 300–8). Latinized as Aeneas, he is
the hero of Virgil's *Aeneid*, in which he brings the surviving
Trojans to Italy, a migration that leads to the birth of the
Roman race.

198–9 *His name will be* Aineias . . . *the bed of a mortal man*: Aphrodite
derives the name Aineias from the '*dreadful* (*ainon* in Greek)
pain' of her humiliation in having to go to bed with a mortal;
for similar uses of etymology see *Hy.* 3. 300–74, 375–87,
493–6, and *Hy.* 19. 47. Although she comforts the frightened Ankhises, the goddess makes it clear that he is far
beneath her and that if she had been in her right mind she
would never have slept with him—a point that she spells out
more forcibly at 247–55 below. Her phrasing in 199—
'because I *fell into* the bed of a mortal man'—stresses her
lack of choice.

200–46 *But those who in form and appearance . . . shuddered at even by
gods*: Aphrodite soothes Ankhises' fears by reminding him
that he comes from a family beloved of the gods. Zeus was so
infatuated with Ganymedes (Ankhises' grand-uncle) that he
snatched him up to Olympos, made him immortal, and

appointed him cupbearer of the gods; in case Ankhises gets his hopes up too high, she then turns to Tithonos (his second cousin), who was doomed to an everlasting old age due to the goddess Dawn's botched attempt to make him immortal. Aphrodite expresses unwillingness to risk harming Ankhises in such a manner; but this is hardly the real reason why she does not immortalize him, as she could easily avoid repeating Dawn's mistake. A possible explanation is that Aphrodite, like Dawn, would have to ask Zeus for immortality on behalf of her lover; but Zeus, who causes her to fall in love with this mortal in revenge for all the times that she degraded the other gods in this way, is unlikely to agree (Clay 1989: 190). Aphrodite spares herself the humiliation of pleading for what will be denied.

Clay (1989: 166–70, 198–201) argues that Zeus' purpose is not merely to take revenge on Aphrodite, but to ensure that she discontinues her practice of mating gods with humans and producing half-human, half-divine heroes; in future, the separation between mortals and immortals will be more distinct.

208 *the stormwind sent from heaven*: in later versions Zeus sends an eagle to abduct Ganymedes.

210–17 *Zeus took pity and gave him . . . with hooves moving swift as the storm*: the symmetry of the story is left incomplete: a mortal is taken from earth to Olympos, and in compensation heavenly horses (presumably a pair) are sent down to earth; Ganymedes becomes immortal, but we are not told if the horses succumb to death—the two steeds presented by Poseidon to Peleus and passed on by him to Akhilleus remain immortal despite their subjection to humans (*Iliad* 16. 145–54, 17. 426–58, 19. 399–424, 23. 276–84). At *Iliad* 5. 265–72 Diomedes covets, and subsequently wins in battle, Aineias' horses, which are descended from those that Zeus gives here to Tros (Aineias' great-great-grandfather).

218–38 *And so too by golden-throned Dawn . . . was found in his pliant limbs*: in the Homeric epics Dawn still shares her bed with Tithonos (*Iliad* 11. 1–2; *Odyssey* 5. 1–2). Later sources follow the hymn in ascribing to him an eternal old age, adding that he shrivels into the cicada, a small insect noted for its incessant chirruping. His name, perhaps Anatolian in origin, has been connected with an obscure word *tito* said to mean 'dawn' (Hainsworth 1993: 214). The children of Dawn by Tithonos are Memnon, the last great opponent that Akhilleus slew before his own death (a story told in the post-Homeric epic *Aithiopis*), and the less renowned Emathion (Hesiod, *Theogony* 984–5). Dawn could not resist the transitory charms of mortal men, also abducting at various times Kephalos, Orion, and Kleitos (West 1966: 426). In such myths the love of the goddess represents death, the favoured hero being 'too good for this world'; the practice of holding funerals at night, with the souls of the dead imagined as departing at dawn, may underlie these stories to some degree (Vermeule 1979: 18–21, 162–5; *Iliad* 23. 226–57, 24. 788–803).

237 *From him flows ceaseless speech*: this phrase seems intended to bring to mind the ever-chirruping cicada (*tettix*), into which Tithonos is transformed in other versions of the story. At *Iliad* 3. 150–3 the Trojan elders, too old for battle but excellent speakers, are likened to cicadas.

256–73 *As soon as he sees the Sun's light . . . will bring him up in their care*: see NYMPH. It is fitting that Aineias, the child of a mortal man and an immortal goddess, will be reared by intermediate figures who 'follow neither mortals nor immortal gods' (259). Compare the nymphs who rear Dionysos at *Hy.* 26. 3–10; unlike Dionysos, however, Aineias will not be 'reckoned amongst the immortals' (*Hy.* 26. 6)—not, at least, until the Romans make him the god Indiges (Ovid, *Metamorphoses* 14. 581–608).

274–5 *As soon as upon him comes . . . and show to you the child*: there seems little point in the nymphs showing Ankhises a glimpse of his son when he reaches 'the time of gorgeous youth' (which can hardly refer to a stage earlier than adolescence, given the previous use of the phrase at 225) and then taking him away again, only for Aphrodite to bring him back to his father for good after a further four years have passed (276–7). It may be best to excise 274–5 as an interpolation. If Aphrodite is promising to hand over their son once and for all when he is 4 years old, the hymn will harmonize with *Iliad* 13. 463–7, where Aineias is said to have been reared when little by his brother-in-law, Alkathoos (why Ankhises could not rear his son himself is not stated, but see note on 281–90).

281–90 *If any of mortal men . . . but dread the wrath of the gods*: compare the final admonition in 289–90 with that given by Apollo to the Cretans at *Hy*. 3. 544. In myth such emphatic warnings are often disregarded: in some later sources Ankhises does indeed boast of having slept with Aphrodite, and is either lamed or blinded by Zeus' thunderbolt in punishment (Allen, Halliday, and Sikes 1936: 372).

287 *That you were joined with Kythera's fair-crowned goddess in love*: it is only now that Aphrodite, having given a hint at 249–51, clearly identifies herself to Ankhises, and even still she does not boldly say, 'I am Aphrodite'. Contrast other divine epiphanies, where the declaration of identity is made more directly and proudly (*Hy*. 2. 268–9; *Hy*. 3. 480; *Hy*. 7. 56–7). The poet has altered this standard element of the epiphany to emphasize Aphrodite's shame at her liaison with a mortal.

293 *From you I began; I will now move on to another hymn*: see note on *Hy*. 2. 495.

Hymn 6: *To Aphrodite*

3–5 *There strong Zephyr's moist breath . . . amid the soft foam, to shore*: the hymnist follows the Hesiodic version of Aphrodite's birth, in which the goddess' name is derived from *aphros*, 'foam': see APHRODITE.

21 *But I will call to my mind both you and another song*: see note on *Hy*. 2. 495.

Hymn 7: *To Dionysos*

As with many of the *Hymns*, there is a dearth of firm evidence whereby this poem's date and origin might be ascertained. At a guess, it may belong to the seventh century BC, and its nautical element may imply an origin in Ionia (Janko 1982: 137, 183–4). In content it follows a pattern typical of stories relating to Dionysos: at first the god is unrecognized and maltreated by humans, though a prudent minority protests; he then manifests his power, punishes those who abused him, and declares his identity. Compare Euripides' tragedy *Bakkhai* (*Bacchae*).

3–6   *in looks like a young man whose prime . . . he wore a cloak | Of purple*: Dionysos' disguise is similar to that adopted by Apollo at *Hy.* 3. 449–50. To the pirates the purple robe of the 'young man' would have suggested wealth, as purple dye was expensive.

8   *Tyrsenians*: this name (*Tyrsenoi* in the Greek) perhaps refers to the piratical inhabitants of Lemnos and Imbros, though it can also designate the Etruscans. See Allen, Halliday, and Sikes (1936: 381), West (1966: 435–6), and Càssola (1975: 562–3). Concerning piracy, see note on *Hy.* 2. 125.

13–14   *But their bonds could not hold him, far | From his hands and feet the withies kept falling*: see note on *Hy.* 4. 409–14.

14–15   *And with his dark eyes smiled*: this enigmatic smile is characteristic of Dionysos: see Euripides' *Bakkhai* 380, 439, 1021.

19–20   *For Zeus is here, or Apollo, God of the Silver Bow, | Or Poseidon*: the helmsman recognizes that the prisoner is a god, but cannot tell which god he is. His omission of Dionysos' name from the list of possible deities suggests (but does not prove) that this story, like many of the myths involving Dionysos, is set in the period when he is spreading his worship for the first time amongst humans. (Contrast Ankhises' inclusion of Aphrodite's name in his speculative list at *Hy.* 5. 92–9.)

35–48   *Wine at first began . . . the men fled back to the stern*: the proliferation of vine and ivy, the flowing of streams of wine, the transformation of the god into a lion, and the sudden appearance of other wild animals such as the bear, are all paralleled elsewhere in Dionysiac myth. Compare Euripides' *Bakkhai* 704–11, where the frenzied followers of the god are able to make streams of water, wine, and milk spring up from the ground, and their wands ooze honey; and *Bakkhai* 1017–19, where a bull, a many-headed snake, and a lion are listed as possible manifestations of Dionysos.

56–7   *I am Dionysos who roars . . . who was joined in love with Zeus*: concerning the declaration of identity, see note on *Hy.* 3. 480; concerning the expression 'joined in love with', see note on *Hy.* 4. 4. The god's description of himself as one 'who roars out loud' is apt, given his frequent adoption of animal avatars such as the bull and lion (see note on 35–48 above, and also *Hy.* 26. 1, 10).

58–9 *It cannot be* | *That one forgetful of you arrays a song that is sweet*:
see note on *Hy.* 2. 495.

Hymn 8: *To Ares*

The association of Ares with the planet Mars (6–8), and the para-
doxical plea to the god of war for the ability to restrain oneself from
entering battle (14–17), are among the features that mark this hymn as
unhomeric. West (1970: 303–4) has argued persuasively that it was
included in the collection of Homeric hymns through an accident of
binding in a medieval manuscript, and properly belongs among the
hymns of the Neoplatonist philosopher Proclus, who lived in the fifth
century AD.

8 *beyond the third rim*: this phrase (to which I have added in
the translation the words 'of the sky', in order to clarify the
sense), together with the reference in the previous verse to
'seven paths', suggests that the hymnist subscribed to a
theory of the heavens similar to that propounded in the
pseudo-Aristotelian work *On the Universe* (*de Mundo*, 392^{a}5–
31). In this theory the Earth is surrounded by seven circles,
in each of which a planet moves; enclosing the Earth and
these seven circles is a sphere that contains the fixed stars.
In the first circle (the outermost from the Earth, and
nearest to the sphere of fixed stars) is the planet Saturn;
in the second, Jupiter; in the third, Mars; in the fourth,
Mercury; in the fifth, Venus; in the sixth, the Sun; and in
the circle nearest to the Earth, the Moon. Certain other
ancient sources, while differing from this model in some
respects, agree in putting Mars in the third circle, as does
the poet of *Hy.* 8. See Allen, Halliday, and Sikes (1936:
387–8).

Hymn 9: *To Artemis*

8–9 *But you are my song's first theme . . . move on to another hymn*: see
note on *Hy.* 2. 495.

Hymn 10: *To Aphrodite*

2 *soothing gifts*: i.e. sexual pleasure.

6 *But I will call to my mind both you and another song*: see note on
Hy. 2. 495.

Hymn 12: *To Hera*

This poem lacks a proper hymnic conclusion (Janko 1981: 15–16).

Hymn 13: *To Demeter*

This, the shortest of the *Hymns*, consists merely of an introduction and conclusion, with no intervening middle section (Janko 1981: 10–11, 15–16). It appears to be derived from *Hy.* 2, in that they share the same opening verse, and *Hy.* 13. 2 seems to be adapted from *Hy.* 2. 493; but the priority of the longer poem cannot be proven. Both could be independently indebted to earlier tradition, or could be the work of the same poet, varying the length of his prelude to suit the circumstances of his recitation. Compare *Hy.* 18. 1–9, 10 with *Hy.* 4. 1–9, 579.

Hymn 14: *To the Mother of the Gods*

The goddess to whom this hymn is dedicated is sometimes identified with Rhea (in many manuscripts the hymn's title is *To Rhea*), Earth (called 'Mother of Gods' at *Hy.* 30. 17), or Demeter; she was also worshipped as Kybele, an Anatolian name that might reflect an Asiatic origin of the cult, though perhaps the Anatolian Kybele was merged with a pre-existing Greek Great Mother figure. As in the hymn (3–5), she is often associated with mountains, wild animals, and an ecstatic style of worship that features rattles, drums, and flutes (and that climaxes in the self-castration of her priest in Poem 63 of Catullus). See Burkert (1985: 177–9).

Hymn 15: *To Herakles the Lionheart*

   3 *having joined with*: see note on *Hy.* 4. 4.

   6 *He did much that was reckless himself*: Herakles' misdeeds include killing Megara (his first wife) and their children in a fit of madness; murdering his friend Iphitos in fury when the latter's sister Iole is not given to him in marriage; and wrestling with Apollo when he goes to consult the god at Delphi (Zeus breaks up the fight).

Hymn 17: *To the Sons of Zeus*

   4 *After being in secret tamed under*: the metaphor of 'taming' in relation to sexual intercourse is common in Homeric poetry; a virgin is 'untamed' (*Hy.* 2. 145, *Hy.* 5. 82). The secrecy surrounding the conception of Kastor and Polydeukes parallels the surreptitious conception and birth of Zeus'

other illegitimate sons, its motive being to avoid Hera's jealous wrath (see e.g. *Hy.* 1. 7).

Hymn 18: *To Hermes*

Concerning the relation between this poem and *Hy.* 4, see note on *Hy.* 13.

    4 *having joined in love with*: see note on *Hy.* 4. 4.

    11 *From you I began; I will now move on to another hymn*: see note on *Hy.* 2. 495.

Hymn 19: *To Pan*

This is probably one of the later hymns in the collection, showing in its language some possible reminiscences of *Hy.* 4, the latest of the longer hymns. The worship of Pan began to spread from its Arkadian heartland to the rest of Greece near the end of the sixth century BC; the deity may have made his tardy entry into the Homeric poetic tradition through this hymn in the period 500–450 BC. See Janko (1982: 184–5).

    15 *his pipes*: this instrument, now known as the 'pan-pipes', is invented by Hermes, Pan's father, at *Hy.* 4. 511–12.

    17 *that bird*: the nightingale. Her song is a 'dirge' (18) because originally she was a mortal woman who killed her own son (see *Odyssey* 19. 518–23).

  32–3 *There, though a god, he pastured a mortal's rough-fleeced flocks*: Apollo similarly tended the herds of the human Admetos, though this was a punishment imposed upon him by Zeus rather than part of an amorous escapade.

    34 *to be joined in love with*: see note on *Hy.* 4. 4.

    43 *With hides of the mountain hare*: the hare is associated with Pan on coinage, and one of his characteristic implements is the *lagobolon*, a throwing-stick used in the hunting of this animal.

    47 *And* Pan *was the name that they gave him for pleasing the hearts of them* all: the poet derives the name Pan from the Greek word for 'all', but the correct derivation is from a root shared with the Latin verb *pascere*, 'to feed, pasture'— Pan, the god of herdsmen, tends to the needs of the flocks. For similar attempts to explain the origin of names and titles see *Hy.* 3. 371–4, 385–7, 493–6, and *Hy.* 5. 198–9.

49 *But I will call to my mind both you and another song*: see note on
    Hy. 2. 495.

Hymn 21: *To Apollo*

This poem resembles *Hymns* 24 and 29 in opening with the vocative of
the deity's name: either the proper openings of these poems have been
shorn away, or this use of the vocative of the deity's name constitutes 'a
rare sub-type' of the hymnic introduction (Janko 1981: 10).

3–4 *and of you* | *The sweet bard with clear-sounding lyre sings ever both
     first and last*: see note on *Hy.* 2. 495.

Hymn 23: *To Zeus*

2 *Themis*: according to Hesiod (*Theogony* 901), Themis, who is
   Righteousness personified, was the second wife of Zeus
   (after Metis, 'Craft').

Hymn 24: *To Hestia*

Concerning the opening of this hymn, see note on *Hy.* 21.

1–2 *Hestia, you who at holy . . . Apollo who shoots from afar*:
     concerning this association of Hestia with Apollo, and her
     presence in other gods' shrines, see notes on *Hy.* 5. 24, 29–
     32; compare also *Hy.* 29. 1–6.

3 *The locks of your hair are always dripping with liquid oil*: olive oil
   had many uses in antiquity, including the treatment of hair.
   At *Iliad* 23. 281–2 it is said that Patroklos used to wash and
   then pour oil on the manes of Akhilleus' horses.

4–5 *Enter this house, your heart . . . your favouring grace besides*: the
     poet invites the goddess to enter the 'house' where he is
     singing; it is impossible to say what sort of building is meant.
     It might be an aristocratic home where a feast is being held,
     or a temple that is being dedicated (Allen, Halliday, and
     Sikes 1936: 418).

Hymn 25: *To the Muses, Apollo, and Zeus*

2–5 *For it is from the Muses and lord . . . is the voice that flows from his
     lips*: these verses are excerpted from Hesiod's *Theogony* (94–
     7), the influence of which is also apparent in verses 1 and 6
     (cf. *Theogony* 1, 104).

7 *But I will call to my mind both you and another song*: see note on
   Hy. 2. 495.

Hymn 26: *To Dionysos*

 1 *With the god who has ivy hair, Dionysos who roars out loud*: ivy, evergreen and prolific, is as much associated with Dionysos as is the vine; see *Hy.* 7. 40–2. For the god's description as one 'who roars out loud' (fully justified by 10 below) see note on *Hy.* 7. 56–7.

 3–9 *He was reared by nymphs whose tresses are fair . . . covered with ivy and bay*: like Aineias at *Hy.* 5. 256–73, Dionysos is handed over by his divine parent to mountain nymphs for rearing; unlike Aineias, he is 'reckoned amongst the immortals' (6). Like Hermes in *Hy.* 4, he is reared within a cave, from which he departs to spread his renown through the world.

 9–10 *Behind him followed the nymphs . . . the forest rang with his roar*: in literary and artistic depictions Dionysos is often attended by a *thiasos* or band of Maenads, frenzied female worshippers.

 12–13 *Permit us to come once more . . . for many succeeding years*: these verses imply that the festival of Dionysos at which the hymn was recited was held annually: contrast *Hy.* 1. 11–12.

Hymn 27: *To Artemis*

 1 *with distaff of gold, whose cry resounds*: many, finding it inconceivable that Artemis, the virgin huntress, could have a distaff as one of her characteristic possessions, interpret the word *khruselakatos* as 'with arrows of gold'. If this is correct, the original sense was lost at an early stage, as it refers to the distaff at *Odyssey* 4. 120–35. See Heubeck, West, and Hainsworth (1988: 201) and Janko (1992: 343). The expression 'whose cry resounds' probably refers to the cry of the hunt.

 22 *But I will call to my mind both you and another song*: see note on *Hy.* 2. 495.

Hymn 28: *To Athena*

 4 *Craft-filled Zeus*: I usually translate *metieta* as 'sagacious', but here and in 16 prefer 'Craft-filled', as the poet is referring to Metis ('Craft'). See note on *Hy.* 3. 322–5[a] and ATHENA; cf. Dionysos' birth from Zeus' thigh (*Hy.* 1. 6–7).

 13–14 *and Hyperion's splendid son . . . the swift hoofs of his chariot's team*: see note on *Hy.* 31. 14.

18 *But I will call to my mind both you and another song*: see note on
    Hy. 2. 495.

Hymn 29: *To Hestia*

This hymn is dedicated as much to Hermes as to Hestia: compare
Hy. 24. 1–2, where she is associated with Apollo, and *Hy.* 24. 5, where
she is linked with Zeus; see also *Hy.* 5. 29–32. It is in Hestia's nature to
be worshipped jointly with other gods. Her association here with
Hermes may be based on the latter's role both as sender of dreams
and as watcher at gates (see notes on *Hy.* 4. 14, 15). 'Hestia represented
the religious focus of the family life at meals, and Hermes was the
protector of the sleep of the family . . . At bedtime Hermes usurped the
prerogative of the last libation, which at other times of the day belonged
to Hestia' (Allen, Halliday, and Sikes 1936: 428). But it has also been
suggested that the hymn was performed at the dedication of a new
building, such as a gymnasium, palaestra, aristocratic dwelling, or a
temple belonging jointly to Hestia and Hermes (Càssola 1975: 425).
Concerning the opening of this hymn, see note on *Hy.* 21.

4–6 *for not without you\Are banquets . . . for Hestia first and last*: the
     phrasing of the Greek here seems slightly awry, implying
     that in banquets where Hestia is absent she is honoured with
     the first and last of the libations at the start of the festivity;
     what the poet is trying to say is both that banquets cannot be
     held without Hestia being present, and that there are no
     banquets in which she does not receive these libations.

6 *pours out\No wine as sweet as honey*: i.e. as a libation (drink-
   offering).

9–12 *Being gracious, bring me your help . . . you attend on thought and
      youth*: the Greek text here is problematic; the sense adopted
      in the translation results from a reordering of verses (putting
      9 after 11) and the emendation of a word (to give 'props',
      12). See Càssola (1975: 584–5).

14 *But I will call to my mind both you and another song*: see note on
    Hy. 2. 495.

Hymn 30: *To Earth the Mother of All*

5–16 *From you comes abundance of children . . . bountiful power, you
      give*: the man favoured by Earth enjoys the same blessings
      that Ankhises asks of Aphrodite at *Hy.* 5. 102–6; initiates in
      the Eleusinian Mysteries are also promised material com-

forts in this life, but they can look forward to a better lot in death as well (*Hy.* 2. 480–2, 486–9).

19 *But I will call to my mind both you and another song*: see note on *Hy.* 2. 495.

Hymn 31: *To the Sun*

Hy. 31 and *Hy.* 32 are very similar, and may be the work of the same poet. Both are 'somewhat florid in style' (Allen, Halliday, and Sikes 1936: 431). Although firm evidence for assigning a date to them is lacking, they do not belong amongst the earliest of the *Hymns*.

2 *cow-eyed*: this epithet is usually applied to Hera (see note on *Hy.* 3. 332).

14 *The stallions below*: a lacuna has swallowed up the description of the Sun's ascent to the zenith at noon, the time when 'he brings to a halt his gold-yoked car and his steeds, 'And in godly splendour through heaven sends toward Ocean his team' (15–16). The Sun's horses are stallions, fiery animals for a fiery master; the Moon's chariot is also drawn by male horses, but they are colts (*Hy.* 32. 9), perhaps explaining her wayward course. The Sun appears with horses and chariot also at *Hy.* 2. 62–89, *Hy.* 4. 68–9, and *Hy.* 28. 13–14. The horses of both Sun and Moon are probably imagined as winged—at *Hy.* 2. 89 the Sun's are compared to 'birds with their wings outstretched'. The Sun and Moon (who herself has wings at *Hy.* 32. 1) are not the only deities with flying horses and chariot (see e.g. *Hy.* 2. 16–20, 375–85), but unlike most other gods they have to rely on their animals and vehicles for their daily occupation; the consequences if the Sun's chariot in particular were to go astray would be catastrophic, as the myth of Phaethon shows. A chariot and team of four horses were hurled annually into the sea for the Sun at Rhodes, his main cult centre; the famous 'Colossus of Rhodes' was a bronze statue of the Sun (Burkert 1985: 175).

18–19 *From you I began; I will now . . . the gods have to mortals revealed*: these verses, together with *Hy.* 32. 18–20, make explicit the nature of the *Hymns* as preludes to the recitation of heroic poetry; as such explicitness is lacking in the other hymns, it may be evidence of the relative lateness of *Hy.* 31 and *Hy.* 32 (see note on *Hy.* 2. 495).

Hymn 32: *To Selene*

This poem is a companion-piece to *Hy.* 31.

    1 *to sing*: this infinitive follows on awkwardly from 'give utterance', and may be the product of textual corruption.

    9 *Her long-necked, dazzling colts*: see note on *Hy.* 31. 14.

  14 *was joined*: see note on *Hy.* 4. 4.

18–20 *From you I begin; I will now . . . of the Muses' attendants, the bards*: see notes on *Hy.* 2. 495, *Hy.* 31. 18–19.

Hymn 33: *To the Sons of Zeus*

    5 *having joined in love With*: see note on *Hy.* 4. 4.

 7–17 *When wintry tempests rage . . . and with dismal toil have done*: Horace (*Odes* 1. 12. 25–32) offers a similar picture of Kastor and Polydeukes' miraculous intervention at sea. Their saving presence during storms was thought to be signalled by the appearance of St Elmo's fire about the ship's mast.

  13 *on rustling wings*: the Moon too is winged at *Hy.* 32. 1.

  16 *and mark their freedom from toil*: the sense here is uncertain, as the Greek text seems to be corrupt.

  19 *But I will call to my mind both you and another song*: see note on *Hy.* 2. 495.

To Hosts

This poem, an appeal for hospitality, does not properly belong with the *Hymns*, but among Homer's 'epigrams'. 'It is perhaps not too much to suppose that the person who made the collection of the Hymns appended it at the end as a sort of *envoi* to the poems in the character of their nominal author' (Allen, Halliday, and Sikes 1936: 442).

    2 *the steep city of Hera*: Kyme, a town in Aiolis on the west coast of Asia Minor.

 4–5 *the yellow stream Of finely flowing Hermos*: Hermos' waters were fabled to be rich with gold, which may explain the colour of its stream here.

GLOSSARY OF NAMES

Hy. = *Hymn*. A name in capital letters refers to another entry in the Glossary. If a name occurs ten or more times within a hymn, only the first occurrence is listed. The Glossary excludes instances where for the sake of clarity a proper name has been introduced into the translation that does not occur in the Greek text.

Admete (*Hy.* 2. 421): 'Untamed' (i.e. virgin), a daughter of Ocean.

Agamedes (*Hy.* 3. 296): a son of Erginos; with his brother Trophonios he lays the threshold of Apollo's shrine at Delphi.

Aïdoneus (*Hy.* 2. 2, 84, 357, 376): see HADES.

Aigai (*Hy.* 3. 32; *Hy.* 22. 3): a name applied to several places in Greece. In *Hy.* 3 an island near Euboia may be meant; in *Hy.* 22, a town in Akhaia in northern Peloponnesos.

Aigina (*Hy.* 3. 31): an island in the Saronic gulf, south of Athens.

aigis (*Hy.* 4. 183, 396, 551; *Hy.* 5. 8, 23, 27, 187; *Hy.* 28. 7, 17): a fearsome piece of equipment used by (most commonly) Zeus and Athena; it has passed into English in the Latinized form *aegis*. Indestructible, it is worn about the shoulders; its decorations include a hundred golden tassels and a Gorgon's head (*Iliad* 2. 446–9, 5. 738–42). The Greeks seem to have viewed it as a goatskin, deriving its name from *aix* (stem *aig-*), 'goat'; some suggest that originally it was the thunderbolt, which would explain its association with Zeus, the sky god (Janko 1992: 230, 260–1).

Aineias (*Hy.* 5. 198): son of Aphrodite and Ankhises. See notes on *Hy.* 5. 196–7, 198–9.

Ainienes (*Hy.* 3. 217): a people perhaps thought of as living in the vicinity of Thessaly in northern Greece (they shifted their abode in the course of time).

Aiolos (*Hy.* 3. 37): King of the Winds. See *Odyssey* 10. 1–76.

Aipy (*Hy.* 3. 423): a town of uncertain location in western Peloponnesos; its name means 'Steep'.

Aisagea (*Hy.* 3. 40): a mountain of uncertain location; perhaps near Klaros in Asia Minor.

Akaste (*Hy.* 2. 421): a daughter of Ocean.

Alkmene (*Hy.* 15. 3): wife of Amphitryon king of Thebes, and mother of Herakles by Zeus.

Alpheios (*Hy.* 1. 3; *Hy.* 3. 423; *Hy.* 4. 101, 139, 398): a river that rises in Arkadia and reaches the sea in western Peloponnesos.

ambrosia (*Hy.* 2. 49, 237; *Hy.* 3. 124; *Hy.* 4. 248; *Hy.* 5. 232): see NEKTAR.

Amphitrite (*Hy.* 3. 94): a sea-goddess; according to Hesiod (*Theogony* 243, 930), a daughter of Nereus and wife of Poseidon.

Ankhises (*Hy.* 5. 53, *passim*): a Trojan prince (great-grandson of Tros) loved by Aphrodite; their child is Aineias.

Antron (*Hy.* 2. 491): a town in Thessaly.

Aphrodite (*Hy.* 2. 102; *Hy.* 3. 195; *Hy.* 5. 1, *passim*; *Hy.* 6. 1): the goddess of love. In the *Iliad* (5. 370–1) she is the daughter of Zeus and Dione; in Hesiod's *Theogony* (188–206) she is born from the foam of the sea into which Kronos threw his castrated father's genitals (*aphros* is Greek for foam). Her two most famous sites of worship were at Paphos on Cyprus (where she was born, or—according to Hesiod— first washed ashore) and Kythera (past which she swept en route to Cyprus, according to Hesiod). Hence she is 'the Cyprian', 'the Native of Cyprus', 'Kythera's goddess'. In the *Odyssey* (8. 266–366) her husband is Hephaistos, her lover Ares; in *Hy.* 5 Zeus makes her fall in love with the Trojan Ankhises, by whom she has a mortal son, Aineias.

Apollo (*Hy.* 3. 1, *passim*; *Hy.* 4. 18, *passim*; *Hy.* 5. 24, 151; *Hy.* 7. 19; *Hy.* 9. 2, 5; *Hy.* 16. 2; *Hy.* 24. 1; *Hy.* 25. 1, 2; *Hy.* 27. 3, 14): called *Apollon* in Greek, he is the son of Zeus and Leto, and brother of Artemis. The island of Delos was held to be his birthplace. A famous archer, through his arrows he makes his fatal influence felt from afar: hence two of his commonest titles, 'Far-shooter' and 'Far-worker'. He is a god of prophecy (his most famous oracle was at Delphi: see PYTHO), of music (the lyre was especially associated with him), and of healing (he is father of Asklepios). He came to be identified with the Sun, though this is not apparent in Homer. 'Phoibos' is a name frequently applied to him.

Arene (*Hy.* 3. 422): a town on the coast of western Peloponnesos.

Ares (*Hy.* 3. 200; *Hy.* 5. 10; *Hy.* 8. 1; *Hy.* 11. 2): the god of war, son of Zeus and Hera.

Argos: see SLAYER OF ARGOS.

Argyphea (*Hy.* 3. 422): a place of uncertain location in western Peloponnesos.

Arkadia (*Hy.* 4. 2; *Hy.* 18. 2; *Hy.* 19. 30): a region in central Peloponnesos, where Hermes and Pan were most worshipped. Its inhabitants led a pastoral existence (hence it is called 'the mother of flocks' at *Hy.* 19. 30) and retained many archaic features of language and custom.

Artemis (*Hy.* 2. 424; *Hy.* 3. 15, 159, 165, 199; *Hy.* 5. 16, 93, 118; *Hy.* 9. 1; *Hy.* 27. 1): the virgin huntress goddess, daughter of Zeus and Leto, sister of Apollo, and expert in archery; according to *Hy.* 3. 16, Ortygia was her birthplace. With her arrows she sends sudden death to women, particularly in childbirth.

Asklepios (*Hy.* 16. 1): son of Apollo by Koronis. Apollo, having killed Koronis in anger at her infidelity, rescued their unborn child and gave him to the Centaur Kheiron to rear. Asklepios grew up to become the most skilful of healers; Zeus blasted him with the thunderbolt for raising the dead to life. He was worshipped as a god of healing.

Athena (*Hy.* 3. 308, 314, 323; *Hy.* 5. 8, 94; *Hy.* 11. 1; *Hy.* 20. 2; *Hy.* 28. 1, 16): called *Athene* or *Athenaie* in the Greek text, she is the virgin goddess of wisdom, handicrafts, and defensive war. Both *Hy.* 3. 305–30 and *Hy.* 28 refer to the story of her birth, told more fully by Hesiod (*Theogony* 886–900): Zeus married Metis (Craft/Resource), who became pregnant; warned that Metis would bear a son mightier than his father, Zeus swallowed her; this action prevented the birth of a son, but Athena emerged from her father's brow in full armour. She is often called 'Pallas'.

Athens (*Hy.* 3. 30): *Athenai* in Greek; the chief city of Attike (Attica) in central Greece.

Athos (*Hy.* 3. 33): called *Athoös* in the Greek text, this is a mountain in Thrace, at the end of a promontory jutting into the northern Aegean sea.

Atlas (*Hy.* 18. 4): the Titan who holds up the sky. He is the father of several daughters, one of whom is Maia, Hermes' mother.

Autokane (*Hy.* 3. 35): a mountain in Asia Minor, perhaps opposite the island of Lesbos.

Azan (*Hy.* 3. 209): Arkas, the eponymous king of Arkadia, divided his kingdom between his sons, Azan, Apheidas, and Elatos (Pausanias 8. 4. 1–7). In *Hy.* 3 Azan is the father of an unnamed daughter who was courted by the god Apollo and the mortal Iskhys, Elatos' son; elsewhere it is said that Apollo and Iskhys were rivals for the affections of Koronis, daughter of Phlegyas and mother by Apollo of Asklepios (see *Hy.* 16 and ASKLEPIOS).

Bakkheios (*Hy.* 19. 46): a title of Dionysos, related to his other common name, Bakkhos (Bacchus).

Bestower of Splendid Gifts (*Hy.* 2. 54, 192, 492): a title of Demeter.

Bringer of Seasons (*Hy.* 2. 54, 192, 492): a title of Demeter.

Centaur (*Hy.* 4. 224): *Kentauros* in Greek. Part-human, part-equine, the Centaurs are often portrayed as a brutish race who cannot hold their drink and are prone to abducting women; the noble exception is Kheiron (Chiron), who acts as tutor to many heroes (e.g. Herakles, Akhilleus) and is skilled in healing.

Commander of Many (*Hy.* 2. 31, 84, 376): a title of Hades.

Conductor (*Hy.* 4. 392, 514; *Hy.* 5. 147, 213; *Hy.* 18. 12): a title of Hermes. See note on *Hy.* 4. 392.

Cretans, the (*Hy.* 3. 393, 463, 517, 518, 525): merchants from Crete whose ship is hijacked by Apollo in *Hy.* 3; they become his priests at Delphi.

Crete (*Hy.* 2. 123; *Hy.* 3. 30, 470): *Krete* in Greek, this is the large island south of Greece.

Cyprian, the (*Hy.* 5. 2): see APHRODITE.

Cyprus (*Hy.* 5. 58, 66, 292; *Hy.* 6. 2; *Hy.* 7. 28; *Hy.* 10. 5): *Kypros* in Greek, this is the large island off the south coast of Asia Minor. At *Hy.* 10. 1 the 'Native of Cyprus' (*Kyprogenes* in the Greek text) is Aphrodite.

Dardanos (*Hy.* 5. 177): a son of Zeus, and the founder of the Trojan race. Ankhises is his descendant (his great-great-great-grandson), not literally his 'son'.

Dawn (*Hy.* 2. 51, 293; *Hy.* 3. 436; *Hy.* 4. 184, 326; *Hy.* 5. 218, 223, 226, 230; *Hy.* 31. 6): *Eos* in Greek, daughter of Hyperion and Euryphaëssa, and sister of the Moon and Sun. At *Hy.* 5. 218–38 the story of her love for Tithonos is told.

Delian Women, the (*Hy.* 3. 157): the young women of Delos who sing at Apollo's festival there.

Delos (*Hy.* 3. 16, *passim*): one of the Cyclades islands in the Aegean sea, and the birthplace of Apollo; the Ionians held a festival there in his honour.

Delphi (*Hy.* 27. 14): *Delphoi* in Greek; the site of Apollo's main oracle. See PYTHO.

Delphinios (*Hy.* 3. 495): a title of Apollo. See note on *Hy.* 3. 493–6.

Demeter (*Hy.* 2. 1, *passim*; *Hy.* 13. 1): a daughter of Kronos and Rhea, and mother of Persephone by Zeus. Known also as Deo, she is the goddess of agriculture.

Demo (*Hy.* 2. 109): a daughter of Keleos and Metaneira.

Demophoon (*Hy.* 2. 234, 248): the infant son of Keleos and Metaneira whom Demeter tries to make immortal.

Deo (*Hy.* 2. 47, 211, 492): see DEMETER.

Diokles (*Hy.* 2. 474, 477): see DIOKLOS.

Dioklos (*Hy.* 2. 153): one of the chiefs of Eleusis, probably identical to the 'Diokles' mentioned later in *Hy.* 2.

Dione (*Hy.* 3. 93): a goddess present at the birth of Apollo; in the *Iliad* she is the mother of Aphrodite by Zeus.

Dionysos (*Hy.* 1. 20; *Hy.* 7. 1, 56; *Hy.* 19. 46; *Hy.* 26. 1, 11): the god of wine, son of Zeus and Semele; regarding his birth, see note on *Hy.* 1. 6. In stories about him mortals often fail to recognize his divinity, with disastrous consequences (see *Hy.* 7). Bands of frenzied female followers called Maenads (*Mainades*, 'Madwomen') are a feature of his cult, and in myth they rend asunder his mortal opponents. Apart from the vine, he is also associated with ivy (his hair is ivy at *Hy.* 26. 1), and frequently takes the shape of wild animals (see note on *Hy.* 7. 35–48).

Dolikhos (*Hy.* 2. 155): one of the chiefs of Eleusis.

Doso (*Hy.* 2. 122): 'Giver', Demeter's pseudonym at Eleusis.

Dotion plain, the (*Hy.* 16. 3): in eastern Thessaly in the north of Greece.

Doulikhion (*Hy.* 3. 429): a place near Ithake of uncertain location.

Drakanon (*Hy.* 1. 1): a cape on the island of Kos.

Dryops (*Hy.* 19. 34): a dweller in Arkadia whose daughter bears Hermes' son Pan. His name may be related to *drys*, oak-tree; he is the eponym of a people called the *Dryopes*.

Dyme (*Hy.* 3. 425): a town on the coast of north-western Peloponnesos.

Earth (*Hy.* 2. 9, 14, 16, 33, 428; *Hy.* 3. 84, 118, 334, 341, 365, 369; *Hy.* 4. 427,

570; *Hy.* 5. 227; *Hy.* 28. 10; *Hy.* 30. 1; *Hy.* 31. 3): *Gaia* or *Ge* in Greek (sometimes also *Khthon*). The eldest of the gods, she is the wife of Heaven and the mother of the Titans.

Egypt (*Hy.* 1. 9; *Hy.* 7. 28): *Aigyptos* in Greek.

Eileithyia (*Hy.* 3. 97, 103, 110, 115): the goddess of childbirth.

Eiresiai (*Hy.* 3. 32): a place of uncertain location through which Leto passes.

Elatos (*Hy.* 3. 210): the father of Iskhys; see AZAN.

Elektra (*Hy.* 2. 418): a daughter of Ocean.

Eleusinos (*Hy.* 2. 105): the father of Keleos, and eponym of Eleusis.

Eleusis (*Hy.* 2. 97, 318, 356, 490): a town near Athens, and the site of the Eleusinian Mysteries in honour of Demeter and Persephone.

Elis (*Hy.* 3. 426): a district in north-western Peloponnesos.

Epeioi (*Hy.* 3. 426): the people who inhabited Elis.

Erebos (*Hy.* 2. 335, 349, 409): the realm of Hades.

Erekhtheus (*Hy.* 3. 211): a king of Athens, and Apollo's rival in an unspecified love affair.

Erginos (*Hy.* 3. 297): father of Trophonios and Agamedes.

Euboia (*Hy.* 3. 31, 219): the large island north of Athens.

Eumolpos (*Hy.* 2. 154, 475): 'Good Singer', one of the chiefs of Eleusis. A family called the *Eumolpidai* ('Sons of Eumolpos') supplied a priest in the Eleusinian Mysteries.

Euripos (*Hy.* 3. 222): the narrow strait between Euboia and the mainland.

Europa (*Hy.* 3. 251, 291): mainland Greece, excluding Peloponnesos.

Euryphaëssa (*Hy.* 31. 2, 4): 'Wide-Shining', a daughter of Heaven and Earth; she married her brother Hyperion and bore Dawn, Moon, and Sun (but according to Hesiod, *Theogony* 371–4, Theia, another daughter of Heaven and Earth, is Hyperion's wife).

Eurystheus (*Hy.* 15. 5): a favourite of Hera, who accelerated his birth and retarded that of Herakles when Zeus

(with Herakles in mind) swore that a child descended from him and born on that day would rule over his neighbours. Eurystheus (son of Sthenelos son of Perseus son of Zeus) was born first, and therefore gained the kingship of Argos and Mykenai; Herakles had to perform the Twelve Labours for him. See *Iliad* 19. 95–133.

Far-shooter (*Hy.* 3. 1, *passim*; *Hy.* 4. 18, 218, 234, 236, 417, 509, 522; *Hy.* 5. 151; *Hy.* 9. 1, 6; *Hy.* 24. 1; *Hy.* 25. 2): a title of Apollo; also translated as 'far-shooting' or 'who shoots from afar'. At *Hy.* 9. 6 it is applied to Artemis.

Far-worker (*Hy.* 3. 56, 242, 257, 357, 382, 420, 440, 474; *Hy.* 4. 239, 281, 307, 333, 464, 472, 492, 500): a title of Apollo; also translated as 'who works from afar'.

Father (of men and gods) (*Hy.* 1. 6; *Hy.* 2. 321, 325, 348, 364, 396, 408; *Hy.* 3. 307; *Hy.* 5. 27, 29): a title of Zeus as supreme deity.

Galaxaure (*Hy.* 2. 423): a daughter of Ocean.

Ganymedes (*Hy.* 5. 202): a Trojan prince, the handsome son of Tros, snatched away by Zeus to be the gods' cup-bearer. See note on *Hy.* 5. 200–46.

Giver of Good (*Hy.* 18. 12; *Hy.* 29. 8): a title of Hermes.

God of the Silver Bow (*Hy.* 3. 140, 178; *Hy.* 4. 318, 327; *Hy.* 7. 19; *Hy.* 9. 5): Apollo.

Grace-Giver (*Hy.* 18. 12): a title of Hermes.

Graces, the (*Hy.* 3. 194; *Hy.* 5. 61, 95; *Hy.* 27. 15): called *Kharites* in Greek, these are goddesses personifying grace and beauty.

Hades (*Hy.* 2. 2, 79, 84, 336, 347, 357, 376; *Hy.* 4. 572; *Hy.* 5. 154): called *Aïdes, Haides,* and *Aïdoneus* in the Greek text, he is the god of the dead, and a son of Kronos and Rhea. His abduction of Persephone is one of the few occasions when he leaves the underworld. 'Lord of Those Below', 'Commander of Many', and 'Receiver of Many' are among his titles.

Haliartos (*Hy.* 3. 243): a town in Boiotia in central Greece.

Harmony (*Hy.* 3. 195): a personified abstraction, *Harmonie* in the Greek text.

Heaven (*Hy.* 2. 13, 33; *Hy.* 3. 84, 334; *Hy.* 30. 17; *Hy.* 31. 3): *Ouranos* in Greek (Latinized as *Uranus*); sometimes translated as 'Sky'. Husband of Earth and father of the Titans, he kept his children confined within Earth until Kronos castrated him (Hesiod, *Theogony* 154–210).

Hebe (*Hy.* 3. 195; *Hy.* 15. 8): the goddess Youth, daughter of Zeus and Hera; she became the bride of Herakles after his apotheosis.

Hekate (*Hy.* 2. 25, 52, 59, 438): Persaios' daughter, a goddess associated with the underworld. In *Hy.* 2 she is benign, aiding Demeter and being described as Persephone's 'usher and helper' (440); in later literature she is often a darker figure, linked with magic, dog sacrifices, crossroads, and the moon, and is sometimes identified with Artemis.

Helikon (*Hy.* 22. 3): a mountain in Boiotia in central Greece.

Hephaistos (*Hy.* 3. 317; *Hy.* 4. 115; *Hy.* 20. 1, 5, 8): son of Zeus and Hera (or, in some traditions, of Hera alone), the god of fire, the lame smith and master craftsman of the Olympian deities. At *Iliad* 18. 382–3 his wife is Kharis, 'Grace'; at *Odyssey* 8. 266–366 she is Aphrodite. See headnote on *Hy.* 1.

Hera (*Hy.* 1. 7; *Hy.* 3. 95, 99, 105, 305, 307, 309, 332, 348, 353; *Hy.* 4. 8; *Hy.* 5. 40; *Hy.* 12. 1; *Hy.* 18. 8; *To Hosts* 2): called *Here* in the Greek text, she is the queen of the gods, the daughter of Kronos and Rhea, and the sister and wife of Zeus, who is notoriously unfaithful to her.

Herakles (*Hy.* 15. 1): son of Zeus by Alkmene, wife of Amphitryon king of Thebes. Hated by Hera, he had to submit to the authority of Eurystheus and performed for him the famous Twelve Labours: see EURYSTHEUS. After these and many other adventures he became a god, and was reconciled with Hera, whose daughter Hebe (Youth) he married.

Hermes (*Hy.* 2. 340; *Hy.* 4. 1, *passim*; *Hy.* 5. 148; *Hy.* 18. 1, 12; *Hy.* 19. 1, 28, 36, 40; *Hy.* 29. 13): called *Hermes* or *Hermeias* in the Greek text, he is the son of Zeus and Maia. Born on Mount Kyllene in Arkadia, he is called 'the Kyllenian'; other titles include 'Slayer of Argos', 'Conductor', 'Grace-Giver', 'Giver of Good'. The god of thieves, travellers, heralds, herdsmen, craftsmen, luck, commerce, and boundaries (among other things), he is a prolific inventor (most notably of the lyre), the herald and messenger of the gods (in particular conveying Zeus' messages to Hades), and as *psychopompos* escorts the dead to the underworld. He owns a golden rod, often called by the Latin name *caduceus*, with magical powers (*Hy.* 4. 528–32). Worshipped most in Arkadia, he fathers that other prominent Arkadian deity, Pan.

Hermos (*To Hosts* 5): a river in Asia Minor.

Hestia (*Hy.* 5. 22; *Hy.* 24. 1; *Hy.* 29. 1, 6, 11): called *Hestie* or *Histie* in the Greek text, she is the virgin goddess of the hearth and home, at once the eldest and youngest of the children of Kronos and Rhea—Kronos, having swallowed her first, regurgitated her last (see KRONOS).

Holder of Earth (*Hy.* 4. 187; *Hy.* 22. 6): this is the traditional rendering of *Gaieokhos*, a title of Poseidon, the original meaning of which is uncertain.

Hyperboreans (*Hy.* 7. 29): *Hyperboreoi* means 'those beyond the North Wind (*Boreas*)'; they are supposed to have been devoted to Apollo, and to have regularly sent offerings to him on Delos (Herodotus 4. 32–6).

Hyperion (*Hy.* 2. 26, 74; *Hy.* 3. 369; *Hy.* 28. 13; *Hy.* 31. 4): in Hesiod, and usually in the *Hymns*, this is a Titan, a son of Earth and Heaven, and the Sun's father (see SUN); at *Hy.* 3. 369, however, and usually in the *Iliad* and *Odyssey*, 'Hyperion' is a title of the Sun, perhaps meaning 'the Higher One'.

Iakhe (*Hy.* 2. 419): a daughter of Ocean.

Iambe (*Hy.* 2. 195, 202): a woman of Eleusis whose joking cheers Demeter up. See note on *Hy.* 2. 192–211.

Ianeira (*Hy.* 2. 421): a daughter of Ocean.

Ianthe (*Hy.* 2. 418): a daughter of Ocean.

Ida (*Hy.* 3. 34; *Hy.* 5. 54, 68): *Ide* in Greek, this is a mountain near Troy.

Ie-Paieon (*Hy.* 3. 272, 500, 517): a title of Apollo, and also the name of a song in his honour, from the ritual cry 'ie Paian'. Paian was originally a god of healing distinct from Apollo.

Ikaros (*Hy.* 1. 1): an island in the Aegean sea (also known as Ikaria).

Ikhnaian (*Hy.* 3. 94): a title of Themis. It might mean 'Tracker', appropriate for the personification of Law; but there was a town called *Ikhnai* in Macedonia, so it might refer to a cult of the goddess there.

Ilios (*Hy.* 5. 280): another name for Troy. (There is a related form *Ilion*, often Latinized as *Ilium*.)

Imbros (*Hy.* 3. 36): an island in the north of the Aegean sea.

Inopos (*Hy.* 3. 18): a stream on Delos.

Iolkos (*Hy.* 3. 218): called *Iaolkos* in the Greek text, this is a coastal town of Thessaly in northern Greece.

Ionians (*Hy.* 3. 147, 152): the *Iaones* were a division of the Greek people, comprising the inhabitants of Athens, the Cyclades islands, and Ionia (the central coastal region of Asia Minor). They celebrated a festival in Apollo's honour on Delos, a central location for them and their main cult centre.

Iris (*Hy.* 2. 314; *Hy.* 3. 102, 107): the goddess of the rainbow, and messenger of the gods in both the *Iliad* and *Hymns* 2 and 3.

Iskhys (*Hy.* 3. 210): a mortal, son of Elatos, and Apollo's rival for Azan's daughter in *Hy.* 3; elsewhere the woman whose affections they both crave is Koronis, daughter of Phlegyas and mother by Apollo of Asklepios.

Ithake (*Hy.* 3. 428): an island off the west coast of Greece, famously the home of Odysseus, the hero of Homer's *Odyssey*. (Its name is often Latinized as *Ithaca*.)

Kadmos (*Hy.* 7. 57): a Phoenician, the founder of Thebes, and father by Harmonia of Semele (Dionysos' mother).

Kallidike (*Hy.* 2. 109, 146): the most beautiful of the daughters of Keleos and Metaneira.

Kallikhoros (*Hy.* 2. 272): a spring at Eleusis (perhaps to be identified with the 'Maiden's Well', *Hy.* 2. 99); its name means 'beautiful dancing-place'.

Kalliope (*Hy.* 31. 2): 'Fair-Voiced', a Muse associated with epic poetry.

Kallirhoe (*Hy.* 2. 419): 'Fair-Flowing', a daughter of Ocean.

Kallithoe (*Hy.* 2. 110): 'Fair-Swift', the eldest daughter of Keleos and Metaneira.

Kalypso (*Hy.* 2. 422): a daughter of Ocean (but Atlas' daughter at *Odyssey* 1. 52).

Karpathos (*Hy.* 3. 43): an island to the south of Rhodes.

Kastor (*Hy.* 17. 1; *Hy.* 33. 3): see SONS OF ZEUS, THE.

Keleos (*Hy.* 2. 96, 105, 146, 184, 233, 294, 475): king of Eleusis, and father by Metaneira of Kallidike, Kleisidike, Demo, Kallithoe, and Demophoon.

Kenaion (*Hy.* 3. 219): the north-west point of Euboia.

Kephisian lake, the (*Hy.* 3. 280): Lake Kopais in Boiotia in central Greece, into which the river Kephisos flowed.

Kephisos (*Hy.* 3. 240): a river in central Greece, flowing into Lake Kopais (called 'the Kephisian Lake' at *Hy.* 3. 280) in Boiotia.

Khalkis (*Hy.* 3. 425): a small stream and settlement south of the river Alpheios on the coast of western Peloponnesos.

Khimaira (*Hy.* 3. 368): a monster with three heads (those of a lion, goat, and snake) killed by Bellerophon on Pegasos (Hesiod, *Theogony* 319–25).

Khios (*Hy.* 3. 38, 172): an island in the Aegean sea, near Asia Minor.

Khryseïs (*Hy.* 2. 421): a daughter of Ocean.

Klaros (*Hy.* 3. 40; *Hy.* 9. 5): an oracular shrine of Apollo in Asia Minor, controlled by the nearby town of Kolophon.

Kleisidike (*Hy*. 2. 109): a daughter of Keleos and Metaneira.

Knidos (*Hy*. 3. 43): a town on a promontory in south-west Asia Minor.

Knossos (*Hy*. 3. 393, 475): the town on Crete where Minos ruled.

Koios (*Hy*. 3. 62): a Titan, the father of Leto.

Koronis (*Hy*. 16. 2): daughter of Phlegyas, king of the Lapiths in Thessaly. Pregnant by Apollo with Asklepios, she fell in love with the mortal Iskhys, and was killed by the jealous god, who rescued Asklepios from her womb.

Korykos (*Hy*. 3. 39): a mountain on the coast of Asia Minor, opposite Khios and south of Mimas.

Kos (*Hy*. 3. 42): an island off the south-west coast of Asia Minor.

Krisa (*Hy*. 3. 269, 282, 431, 438, 445): a town near Delphi, destroyed after the First Sacred War (see note on *Hy*. 3. 540–3).

Kronos (*Hy*. 2. 18, 32; *Hy*. 3. 339; *Hy*. 5. 22, 42; *Hy*. 29. 13): the youngest son of Earth and Heaven, and husband of his sister Rhea; he ruled the Titans after overthrowing his father (see HEAVEN). Zeus, Poseidon, Hades, Hera, Demeter, and Hestia are all children of Kronos and Rhea. Fearing that he himself would be overthrown, Kronos swallowed each of them at birth, but a stone was substituted in place of Zeus (the youngest), who defeated his father and his Titan allies and cast them into Tartaros, having forced Kronos to regurgitate all his other offspring (Hesiod, *Theogony* 453–506).

Kronos' son/son of Kronos (*Hy*. 1. 13; *Hy*. 2. 21, *passim*; *Hy*. 3. 308; *Hy*. 4. 6, 57, 214, 230, 312, 323, 367, 395, 575; *Hy*. 5. 220; *Hy*. 15. 3; *Hy*. 17. 4; *Hy*. 18. 6; *Hy*. 23. 4; *Hy*. 32. 2, 14; *Hy*. 33. 5): this usually denotes Zeus (Hades is 'Kronos' son' at *Hy*. 2. 18, 32).

Krounoi (*Hy*. 3. 425): a source and small stream south of the river Alpheios in western Peloponnesos; its name means simply 'Springs'.

Kyllene (*Hy*. 4. 2, 142, 228, 337; *Hy*. 18.

2): a mountain in Arkadia, and the birthplace of Hermes.

Kyllenian (*Hy*. 4. 304, 318, 387, 408; *Hy*. 18. 1; *Hy*. 19. 31): of/on Kyllene. This is usually a title of Hermes, who was born on Mount Kyllene.

Kynthos (*Hy*. 3. 17, 26, 141): a mountain on Delos.

Kythera's goddess (*Hy*. 5. 6, 175, 287; *Hy*. 6. 18; *Hy*. 10. 1): this title, *Kythereia* in the Greek text, denotes Aphrodite. She had a sanctuary on Kythera, an island off the coast of southern Peloponnesos.

Lakonian (*Hy*. 3. 410): of Lakonike, a region in south-eastern Peloponnesos; its chief town was Sparta.

Leda (*Hy*. 17. 3; *Hy*. 33. 2): wife of Tyndareos king of Sparta, mother of Helen, Kastor, Polydeukes, and Klytaimnestra. Zeus visited her in the shape of a swan, and was the true father of at least Helen and Polydeukes.

Lektos (*Hy*. 3. 217): the identification of this place is uncertain; the context seems to demand a location near Pieria.

Lelantos (*Hy*. 3. 220): a plain on the island of Euboia.

Lemnos (*Hy*. 3. 36): an island in the north of the Aegean sea.

Lesbos (*Hy*. 3. 37): an island in the Aegean sea, near the coast of Asia Minor.

Leto (*Hy*. 3. 5, *passim*; *Hy*. 4. 176, *passim*; *Hy*. 5. 93; *Hy*. 27. 19, 21): daughter of the Titans Koios and Phoibe, and mother by Zeus of Apollo and Artemis.

Leukippe (*Hy*. 2. 418): a daughter of Ocean; her name means 'White Horse'. Water gods are frequently linked with the horse, and even today the white-crested waves of the sea are called 'white horses' (West 1966: 265; Richardson 1974: 288).

Leukippos (*Hy*. 3. 212): 'White Horse', Apollo's rival in a love affair. Elsewhere the god and he are both said to love Daphne, but this does not suit the reference to a 'spouse' of Leukippos at *Hy*. 3. 212, since Daphne does not become his wife (nor Apollo's—she escapes the god's clutches by becoming the bay-tree).

Lilaia (*Hy.* 3. 241): a town north of Delphi in central Greece, near where the river Kephisos rises.

Lord of Those Below (*Hy.* 2. 357): a title of Hades.

Lykia (*Hy.* 3. 179): a region in south-western Asia Minor.

Maenad (*Hy.* 2. 386): *Mainas* in Greek. See DIONYSOS.

Maia (*Hy.* 4. 1, *passim*; *Hy.* 18. 3, 10; *Hy.* 29. 7): called *Maia* or *Maias* in the Greek text, she is a nymph, one of Atlas' daughters. In her cave on Kyllene she mated with Zeus and bore their son, Hermes.

Makar (*Hy.* 3. 37): 'Blessed', Aiolos' son. He was reputed to have been the leader of the first Greeks to settle on Lesbos.

Maleia (*Hy.* 3. 409): a promontory of south-eastern Peloponnesos.

Megamedes (*Hy.* 4. 100): the father of Pallas and grandfather of Selene.

Meionie (*Hy.* 3. 179): a part of Lydia in western Asia Minor.

Meles (*Hy.* 9. 3): a river flowing by Smyrna in western Asia Minor; Homer was said to have been born by its banks.

Melite (*Hy.* 2. 419): a daughter of Ocean; her name is derived from *meli*, 'honey'.

Melobosis (*Hy.* 2. 420): 'Feeder of flocks', a daughter of Ocean.

Meropes (*Hy.* 3. 42): the name of a people dwelling on Kos.

Metaneira (*Hy.* 2. 161, 206, 212, 234, 243, 255): queen of Eleusis, Keleos' wife, mother of Kallidike, Kleisidike, Demo, Kallithoe, and Demophoon; she employs the disguised Demeter as Demophoon's nurse.

Miletos (*Hy.* 3. 42, 180): a city in south-western Asia Minor.

Mimas (*Hy.* 3. 39): a mountain on the coast of Asia Minor, opposite Khios.

Minos (*Hy.* 3. 393): the king of Knossos on Crete.

Mnemosyne (*Hy.* 4. 429): the goddess Memory. A daughter of Earth and Heaven, she mated with Zeus for nine nights and gave birth to nine daugh-

ters—the Muses (Hesiod, *Theogony* 53–62, 135, 915–17).

Moon: see SELENE.

Mother (of All/of Gods) (*Hy.* 14. 1; *Hy.* 30. 1, 17): see note on *Hy.* 14.

Muse(s) (*Hy.* 3. 189, 518; *Hy.* 4. 1, 430, 450; *Hy.* 5. 1; *Hy.* 9. 1; *Hy.* 14. 2; *Hy.* 17. 1; *Hy.* 19. 1; *Hy.* 20. 1; *Hy.* 25. 1, 2, 4; *Hy.* 27. 15; *Hy.* 31. 1; *Hy.* 32. 1, 20; *Hy.* 33. 1): the Muses (*Mousai* in Greek) are the daughters of Zeus and Mnemosyne (Memory). They are nine in number, and one of them, Kalliope, is invoked by name at *Hy.* 31. 2 (see Hesiod, *Theogony* 77–8, for the names of the other eight). Their province includes music, song, poetry, dancing, and eloquence.

Mykale (*Hy.* 3. 41): a mountain on Asia Minor's west coast, facing Samos.

Mykalessos (*Hy.* 3. 224): a town in Boiotia in central Greece.

Naxos (*Hy.* 1. 2; *Hy.* 3. 44): one of the Cyclades islands in the Aegean sea.

nektar (*Hy.* 2. 49; *Hy.* 3. 10, 124; *Hy.* 4. 248; *Hy.* 5. 206): nektar and ambrosia are the food of the gods, the former usually a drink, the latter solid food. See note on *Hy.* 2. 237–41.

Nereus (*Hy.* 3. 319): the Old Man of the Sea, a son of Pontos (Sea). He begot by Doris (a child of Ocean) fifty daughters, the Nereids, including Amphitrite and Thetis (Hesiod, *Theogony* 233–64).

nymph (*Hy.* 4. 4, 7, 60, 229, 244, 250; *Hy.* 5. 97, 98, 119, 257, 284; *Hy.* 18. 7; *Hy.* 19. 3, 19; *Hy.* 26. 3, 10; *To Hosts* 2): *numphe* in Greek. Nymphs are usually a type of lesser goddess (though Hera herself is called a 'nymph' at *To Hosts* 2) associated with mountains, woods, springs, rivers, and the sea. They were especially venerated in rural areas. The role of nymphs in myth is to be loved by major gods (*numphe* in Greek can mean 'bride') and to bear and rear their children; they also provide more important deities with a retinue of obedient subordinates ever ready to sing and dance. They are not always immortal: at *Hy.* 5. 256–73 the nymphs on Mount Ida are linked to trees that sprouted at their birth—when the tree dies, so too does the nymph.

Nysa (*Hy.* 1. 8; *Hy.* 26. 5): the mountain where nymphs rear Dionysos; its location is much disputed, but at *Hy.* 1. 8–9 it is in or near Egypt.

Nysion plain, the (*Hy.* 2. 17): the scene of Persephone's abduction by Hades. Its location is uncertain; it is usually linked to the equally elusive Mount Nysa.

Ocean (*Hy.* 2. 5; *Hy.* 4. 68, 185; *Hy.* 5. 227; *Hy.* 31. 16; *Hy.* 32. 7): *Okeanos* in Greek, a son of Earth and Heaven, pictured as a river encircling the Earth.

Okalea (*Hy.* 3. 242): a town in Boiotia in central Greece.

Okyrhoe (*Hy.* 2. 420): 'Swift-Flowing', a daughter of Ocean.

Olympian (*Hy.* 2. 135, 312; *Hy.* 3. 112; *Hy.* 4. 445, 450; *Hy.* 7. 21; *Hy.* 17. 2): of/on Olympos.

Olympos (*Hy.* 1. 15; *Hy.* 2. 92, 331, 341, 449, 484; *Hy.* 3. 98, 109, 186, 216, 498, 512; *Hy.* 4. 322, 325, 505; *Hy.* 8. 3; *Hy.* 12. 4; *Hy.* 15. 7; *Hy.* 19. 27; *Hy.* 28. 9): a mountain in northern Greece, home of the Olympian gods led by Zeus.

Onkhestos (*Hy.* 3. 230; *Hy.* 4. 88, 186, 190): a town in Boiotia in central Greece, the site of a precinct of Poseidon; at *Hy.* 3. 229–38 a rite practised there is described.

Ortygia (*Hy.* 3. 16): 'Quail Island', the birthplace of Artemis, of uncertain location. It is sometimes identified with Delos, but in *Hy.* 3 they are distinct.

Otreus (*Hy.* 5. 111, 146): Aphrodite's fictitious father in her false tale to Ankhises, in which she pretends to be a woman from Phrygia. Otreus is the name of a Phrygian leader at *Iliad* 3. 186.

Ourania (*Hy.* 2. 423): 'Heavenly', a daughter of Ocean.

Pallas (1) (*Hy.* 2. 424; *Hy.* 11. 1; *Hy.* 28. 1, 16): a title of Athena.

Pallas (2) (*Hy.* 4. 100): Megamedes' son, and father of Selene (but elsewhere he is the Titan Krios' son, Selene's cousin rather than father: Hesiod, *Theogony* 375–6).

Pan (*Hy.* 19. 5, 47): Hermes' son, a god of herdsmen and hunting, in form part-human, part-goat. His worship originated in Arkadia, his birthplace, but began spreading to the rest of Greece by the fifth century BC. In *Hy.* 19 his mother is an anonymous daughter of Dryops; in some other sources, she is Penelope, wife of Odysseus. Concerning the god's name, see note on *Hy.* 19. 47.

Pandeia (*Hy.* 32. 15): 'All-Bright', the daughter of Zeus and Selene.

Paphos (*Hy.* 5. 59): a town on Cyprus where there was a sanctuary of Aphrodite.

Parnassos (*Hy.* 3. 269, 282, 396, 521; *Hy.* 4. 555): called *Parnesos* in the Greek text, this is a mountain in central Greece overlooking Delphi.

Paros (*Hy.* 2. 491; *Hy.* 3. 44): one of the Cyclades islands in the Aegean sea.

Pelion (*Hy.* 3. 33): a mountain on the coast of Thessaly in northern Greece.

Peloponnesos (*Hy.* 3. 250, 290, 419, 430, 432): southern Greece, connected to the north by the Isthmus of Corinth; its name means 'the island of Pelops'.

Peneios (*Hy.* 21. 3): a river in Thessaly in northern Greece.

Peparethos (*Hy.* 3. 32): an island in the Aegean sea, off the coast of Thessaly in northern Greece.

Perrhaiboi (*Hy.* 3. 218): a people perhaps thought of as living in the vicinity of Thessaly in northern Greece (they shifted their abode in the course of time).

Persaios (*Hy.* 2. 24): called Perses by Hesiod (who celebrates his wisdom, *Theogony* 377), he is Hekate's father by Asteria ('Starry One', sister of Leto).

Persephone/Persephoneia (*Hy.* 2. 56, 337, 348, 359, 360, 370, 387, 405, 493; *Hy.* 13. 2): Zeus and Demeter's daughter, she is abducted by Hades to be his bride. Demeter prevents the crops from growing until she secures her daughter's partial release (for two-thirds of every year) from the underworld.

Phaino (*Hy.* 2. 418): a daughter of Ocean.

Pherai (*Hy.* 3. 427): the identification of

this place is uncertain, but a location in north-western Peloponnesos would suit the context.

Phlegyai (*Hy.* 3. 278): see note on *Hy.* 3. 278–9.

Phlegyas (*Hy.* 16. 3): a son of Ares and eponym of the Phlegyai. His daughter is Koronis, the mother of Asklepios by Apollo.

Phoibos (*Hy.* 3. 20, *passim*; *Hy.* 4. 102, 293, 330, 365, 420, 425, 496; *Hy.* 21. 1; *Hy.* 27. 14): a title of Apollo.

Phoinike (*Hy.* 1. 9): Phoenicia.

Phokaia (*Hy.* 3. 35): a town on the west coast of Asia Minor.

Phorbas (*Hy.* 3. 211): a mortal, Triops' son, Apollo's rival in a love affair.

Phrygia (*Hy.* 5. 112, 137): a region in central Asia Minor.

Pieria (*Hy.* 3. 216; *Hy.* 4. 70, 85, 191): a region in the north of Greece.

Plouto (*Hy.* 2. 422): a daughter of Ocean; her name is derived from *ploutos*, 'wealth'. (The related name *Plouton* came to be applied to Hades, and was Latinized as *Pluto*.)

Ploutos (*Hy.* 2. 489): 'Wealth' personified.

Polydeukes (*Hy.* 17. 1; *Hy.* 33. 3): see SONS OF ZEUS, THE.

Polyxeinos (*Hy.* 2. 154, 477): 'Very Hospitable', one of the chiefs of Eleusis.

Poseidon (*Hy.* 3. 230; *Hy.* 5. 24; *Hy.* 7. 20; *Hy.* 22. 1, 6): called *Poseidaon* in the Greek text, he is a son of Kronos and Rhea, and brother of Zeus; god of the sea, horses, and earthquakes.

Pylian (*Hy.* 3. 398, 424): of Pylos.

Pylos (*Hy.* 3. 398, 424, 470; *Hy.* 4. 216, 342, 355, 398): a town in Peloponnesos. Messenia in south-western Peloponnesos is usually thought to be where Homeric Pylos was situated, but in antiquity Triphylia and Elis, regions to the north of Messenia, each had settlements called Pylos claiming to be the Homeric town. In *Hy.* 4, where Hermes drives cattle towards Pylos, the proximity of the river Alpheios might indicate a location in Triphylia.

Pytheios (*Hy.* 3. 373): a title of Apollo at Delphi. See PYTHO.

Pytho (*Hy.* 3. 183, 372, 390, 517; *Hy.* 4. 178; *Hy.* 24. 2): the usual Homeric name for Delphi, the site in central Greece of Apollo's most famous oracle. See note on *Hy.* 3. 300–74.

Rarion plain, the (*Hy.* 2. 450): a plain near Eleusis, made barren by Demeter's wrath but destined to return to fertility; Rhea alights there on her mission to recall Demeter to Olympos. The ploughing of this plain had a part in Athenian ritual, and the prizes in the Eleusinian Games consisted of grain grown upon it (Richardson 1974: 297–8).

Receiver of Many (*Hy.* 2. 9, 17, 31, 404, 430): a title of Hades.

Rhea (*Hy.* 2. 60, 75, 442, 459; *Hy.* 3. 93; *Hy.* 5. 43; *Hy.* 12. 1): called *Rheie* or *Rheë* in the Greek text, she is a daughter of Earth and Heaven, wife of Kronos, and mother of the senior Olympian gods (Zeus, Poseidon, Hades, Hera, Demeter, Hestia).

Rhenaia (*Hy.* 3. 44): one of the Cyclades islands in the Aegean sea, very close to Delos.

Rhodeia (*Hy.* 2. 419): 'Rosy', a daughter of Ocean.

Rhodope (*Hy.* 2. 422): 'Rosy-Face', a daughter of Ocean.

Saidene (*To Hosts* 3): a mountain above Kyme, a town in Aiolis on the west coast of Asia Minor.

Salamis (*Hy.* 10. 4): this is the name both of an island north of Aigina in the Saronic gulf and of a town on this island; it is also the name of a town on Cyprus. In *Hy.* 10 (*To Aphrodite*) the Cyprian town seems the most suitable identification, given Aphrodite's close association with Cyprus.

Same (*Hy.* 3. 429): an island near Ithake off the west coast of Greece, usually identified with Kephallenia.

Samos (1) (*Hy.* 3. 34): 'Samos the Thracian isle' is Samothrace, an island in the north of the Aegean sea.

Samos (2) (*Hy.* 3. 41): an island in the Aegean sea, south of Khios, close to the western coast of Asia Minor.

Seasons, the (*Hy.* 3. 194; *Hy.* 6. 5, 12): *Horai* in Greek, goddesses of the seasons and growth; at *Hy.* 6. 12 they appear to be two in number.

Seilenoi (*Hy.* 5. 262): wild, hedonistic companions of nymphs and other deities, including Dionysos; they overlap with Satyrs and Centaurs, often to the point of being indistinguishable from them.

Selene (*Hy.* 4. 99, 141; *Hy.* 31. 6; *Hy.* 32. 8, 17): the Moon. She is daughter of Pallas, according to *Hy.* 4. 100; daughter of Hyperion and Euryphaëssa, and sister of Dawn and Sun, according to *Hy.* 31. 4–7; and mother by Zeus of Pandeia, according to *Hy.* 32. 14–16. Like the Sun, she rides through the sky in a horse-drawn chariot.

Semele (*Hy.* 1. 4, 21; *Hy.* 7. 1, 57, 58; *Hy.* 26. 2): Kadmos' daughter, mother by Zeus of Dionysos. See notes on *Hy.* 1. 6, 21.

Shaker of Earth (*Hy.* 22. 4): *Ennosigaios* in Greek, a title of Poseidon.

Sky: see HEAVEN.

Skyros (*Hy.* 3. 35): an island in the Aegean sea, east of Euboia.

Slayer of Argos (*Hy.* 2. 335, 346, 377, 407; *Hy.* 3. 200; *Hy.* 4. 73, 84, 294, 387, 414; *Hy.* 5. 117, 121, 129, 213, 262; *Hy.* 18. 1; *Hy.* 29. 7): *Argeiphontes* in Greek, a title of Hermes, of uncertain derivation. The Greeks understood it to refer to the god's slaying of the hundred-eyed Argos, whom Hera had set guarding Io, one of Zeus' mortal paramours; it may, however, have originally meant 'Dog-Killer' (see note on *Hy.* 4. 145).

Smyrna (*Hy.* 9. 4): a town on the west coast of Asia Minor.

Snake, the (*Hy.* 3. 300): Hera entrusted her monstrous son Typhaon to the care of this huge and savage female serpent that lurked at a spring near Delphi; Apollo, having established the site of his oracle there, kills her, and the rotting of her body gives Delphi its other name, Pytho (see note on *Hy.* 3. 300–74).

son of Kronos: see KRONOS' SON.

Sons of Zeus, the (*Hy.* 33. 1, 9): *Dios Kouroi* in Greek, Latinized as *Dioscuri*, these are Kastor and Polydeukes (whom the Romans called Pollux). Their mother is Leda wife of Tyndareos (hence they are also known as 'the sons of Tyndareos'); Helen and Klytaimnestra are their sisters. Often Polydeukes (a noted boxer) is regarded as the son of Zeus, while Kastor ('tamer of horses') is the son of Tyndareos. At *Odyssey* 11. 298–304 they are said to live and be dead on alternate days. They were thought to intervene on behalf of humans at moments of crisis, such as in battle or storms at sea.

Styx (*Hy.* 2. 259, 423; *Hy.* 3. 85; *Hy.* 4. 519): a river of the underworld, the water of which the gods employ in their most solemn and binding oath (see note on *Hy.* 4. 519). Styx is also a goddess, one of the daughters of Ocean who are picking flowers with Persephone when she is abducted by Hades in *Hy.* 2.

Sun (*Hy.* 2. 26, 35, 62, 64; *Hy.* 3. 71, 371, 374, 411, 413, 436; *Hy.* 4. 68, 197, 371, 381; *Hy.* 5. 105, 256, 272; *Hy.* 31. 1, 7): *Helios* or *Eëlios* in Greek (the latter form predominating in Homeric poetry). According to *Hy.* 31. 2–7, he is the son of Hyperion and Euryphaëssa, and brother of the Dawn (Eos) and Moon (Selene). Driving his horse-drawn chariot across the sky, he shines down on the world, seeing everything (and hence is often appealed to as a witness); descending at evening to Ocean, he was thought either to travel under the earth from west to east or to pass eastward along the river of Ocean in a golden bowl. See HYPERION.

Tainaros (*Hy.* 3. 412): the southernmost promontory of Peloponnesos.

Tartaros (*Hy.* 3. 336; *Hy.* 4. 256, 374): the deepest part of the underworld, where Kronos and the Titans are confined (see Hesiod, *Theogony* 713–35).

Taÿgetos (*Hy.* 17. 3; *Hy.* 33. 4): a mountain range in western Lakonike.

Telphousa (*Hy.* 3. 244, 247, 256, 276, 377, 379, 387): a spring in Boiotia in central Greece. Apollo is minded to build his oracle there, but the spring (who is also a goddess) tricks him into moving on; later, discovering the deceit, Apollo piles a mountain on top of her, and raises an altar near by, so gaining the title *Telphousios*. See note on *Hy*. 3. 244.

Telphousios (*Hy*. 3. 386): a title of Apollo. See TELPHOUSA.

Teumessos (*Hy*. 3. 224): a town in Boiotia in central Greece.

Thebes (*Hy*. 1. 5; *Hy*. 3. 225, 226, 228; *Hy*. 15. 2): called *Thebe* or *Thebai* in the Greek text, this is the main city of Boiotia in central Greece. It was founded by Kadmos; Herakles was born there; it is among the reputed birthplaces of Dionysos (his mother Semele was Kadmos' daughter); and Apollo passes through its site, as yet uninhabited, on the way to Delphi.

Themis (*Hy*. 3. 94, 124; *Hy*. 5. 94; *Hy*. 8. 4; *Hy*. 23. 2): the personification of Law and Righteousness.

Thetis (*Hy*. 3. 319): a sea-goddess, one of the daughters of Nereus. She married the mortal Peleus and bore him a son, Akhilleus (Achilles), the hero of the *Iliad*. When Hera flung her own son, Hephaistos, into the sea in disgust at his lameness, Thetis received him kindly (*Iliad* 18. 394–407; *Hy*. 3. 316–21).

Thorikos (*Hy*. 2. 126): a town near Athens.

Thracian (*Hy*. 3. 33, 34): of Thrace, a region to the north of Greece.

Thryon (*Hy*. 3. 423): a town near the coast of western Peloponnesos, described as 'the ford of Alpheios'.

Thyone (*Hy*. 1. 21): another name for Semele. See note on *Hy*. 1. 21.

Titans (*Hy*. 3. 335): called *Titenes* in the Greek text, these are the children of Earth and Heaven who ruled the universe before the Olympian deities. Hesiod (*Theogony* 132–8) names them as Ocean, Koios, Krios, Hyperion, Iapetos, Theia, Rhea, Themis, Mnemosyne, Phoibe, Tethys, and Kronos; this is not a comprehensive list. Kronos, the youngest, was their chief; he overthrew their oppressive father Heaven,

only to be overthrown himself by his own youngest son Zeus, who imprisoned the Titans (with some exceptions, such as Ocean, Rhea, Themis, Mnemosyne, and Tethys) in Tartaros.

Tithonos (*Hy*. 5. 218): a Trojan prince, brother of Priam (king of Troy in the *Iliad*); the goddess Dawn carries him off to be her lover. See notes on *Hy*. 5. 200–46, 218–38.

Triops (*Hy*. 3. 211, 213): father of Phorbas.

Triptolemos (*Hy*. 2. 153, 474, 477): one of the chiefs of Eleusis. In Athenian myth he received from Demeter corn and the art of agriculture, which he taught to all the world (Richardson 1974: 194–6).

Tritogenes (*Hy*. 28. 4): a title of Athena, obscure in meaning; elsewhere the form *Tritogeneia* is commoner. See Kirk (1985: 394).

Trojan (*Hy*. 5. 103, 114, 196): of/from Troy.

Trophonios (*Hy*. 3. 296): a son of Erginos; with his brother Agamedes he lays the threshold of Apollo's shrine at Delphi. He became a chthonic god delivering oracles underground at Lebadeia in Boiotia: see Pausanias 9. 39. 2–14.

Tros (*Hy*. 5. 207): grandson of Dardanos, and the eponym of the Trojan race; he had three sons, Ilos (the eponym of Ilios, and grandfather of King Priam), Assarakos (grandfather of Ankhises), and Ganymedes.

Troy (*Hy*. 5. 66): *Troia* in Greek, the city in north-western Asia Minor that the Greeks besieged for ten years in the Trojan War; it is also called *Ilios*.

Tykhe (*Hy*. 2. 420): a daughter of Ocean; her name means 'fortune', 'success', or 'chance'.

Tyndareos (*Hy*. 17. 2, 5; *Hy*. 33. 2, 18): king of Sparta, husband of Leda; Helen, Kastor, Polydeukes, and Klytaimnestra are their children (though Zeus is the true father of at least Helen and Polydeukes).

Typhaon/Typhoeus (*Hy*. 3. 306, 352, 367): a monster, also called *Typhon*. In *Hy*. 3 Hera, angered when Zeus gives birth to Athena independently of her, conceives Typhaon in parthenogenesis and entrusts him for rearing to the Snake that Apollo later kills at Delphi. Hesiod (*Theogony* 820–80) describes Typhaon as having a hundred snake-heads sprouting from his shoulders with eyes that flash fire and a bizarre multiplicity of voices; in this version Typhaon is a son of Earth and Tartaros who attempts to overthrow Zeus, only to be defeated by him in single combat and thrown into Tartaros, where he is the source of ill winds. In *Hy.* 3 Typhaon's career after his rearing by the Snake is not revealed (except that he caused humans much harm, 355), but a conflict with Zeus is implied (339).

Tyrsenians (*Hy.* 7. 8): see note on *Hy.* 7. 8.

Victory (*Hy.* 8. 4): *Nike* in Greek, the daughter of Ares.

Youth: see HEBE.

Zakynthos (*Hy.* 3. 429): an island off north-western Peloponnesos.

Zephyr (*Hy.* 3. 283, 433; *Hy.* 6. 3): the West Wind, *Zephyros* in Greek.

Zeus (*Hy.* 1. 4, 16; *Hy.* 2. 3, *passim*; *Hy.* 3. 2, *passim*; *Hy.* 4. 1, *passim*; *Hy.* 5. 8, *passim*; *Hy.* 7. 19, 57; *Hy.* 12. 3, 5; *Hy.* 14. 2; *Hy.* 15. 1, 9; *Hy.* 17. 2; *Hy.* 18. 4, 10; *Hy.* 19. 44; *Hy.* 23. 1; *Hy.* 24. 5; *Hy.* 25. 1, 4, 6; *Hy.* 26. 2; *Hy.* 27. 21; *Hy.* 28. 4, 7, 16, 17; *Hy.* 29. 7; *Hy.* 31. 1; *Hy.* 32. 2; *Hy.* 33. 1, 9; *To Hosts* 5): a son of Kronos and Rhea. Overthrowing his father (see KRONOS), he became chief of the Olympian gods and sovereign deity of the universe: hence he is called 'Father of men and gods', or simply 'the Father'. His particular province is the sky, his weapon the thunderbolt: hence he is the 'far-seeing', 'black-clouded', 'deep-crashing', 'loud-thundering' god 'whom thunder delights', 'who gathers the clouds'. His wife is his sister Hera, to whom he is frequently unfaithful. Apart from his siblings (Demeter, Hades, Hera, Hestia, Poseidon), the other main gods (Aphrodite, Apollo, Ares, Artemis, Athena, Dionysos, Hephaistos, Hermes, Persephone) are all his children, together with innumerable lesser gods, goddesses, heroes, and heroines.

*The
Oxford
World's
Classics
Website*

www.worldsclassics.co.uk

- Information about new titles
- Explore the full range of Oxford World's Classics
- Links to other literary sites and the main OUP webpage
- Imaginative competitions, with bookish prizes
- Peruse the Oxford World's Classics Magazine
- Articles by editors
- Extracts from Introductions
- A forum for discussion and feedback on the series
- Special information for teachers and lecturers

www.worldsclassics.co.uk

American Literature

British and Irish Literature

Children's Literature

Classics and Ancient Literature

Colonial Literature

Eastern Literature

European Literature

History

Medieval Literature

Oxford English Drama

Poetry

Philosophy

Politics

Religion

The Oxford Shakespeare

A complete list of Oxford Paperbacks, including Oxford World's Classics, Oxford Shakespeare, Oxford Drama, and Oxford Paperback Reference, is available in the UK from the Academic Division Publicity Department, Oxford University Press, Great Clarendon Street, Oxford OX2 6DP.

In the USA, complete lists are available from the Paperbacks Marketing Manager, Oxford University Press, 198 Madison Avenue, New York, NY 10016.

Oxford Paperbacks are available from all good bookshops. In case of difficulty, customers in the UK can order direct from Oxford University Press Bookshop, Freepost, 116 High Street, Oxford OX1 4BR, enclosing full payment. Please add 10 per cent of published price for postage and packing.